Gabriel Harty OP

D0628083

THE RICHES

VERITAS

First published 1997 by
Veritas Publications
7-8 Lower Abbey Street
Dublin 1

ISBN 1 85390 367 1

British Library Cataloguing
in Publication Data.
A catalogue record for
this book is available
from the British Library.

The paintings reproduced in this book have been used with the permission of Fratelli Alinari, Florence, Italy, and the photographs are copyright © Archivi Alinari/Anderson.

Cover illustration: The Magdalen Reading by Rogier van der Weyden, Flemish, c. 1440.
Reproduced courtesy of the Trustees of the National Gallery, London
*This striking painting shws the two elements in the Rosary, which are highlighted in this book: the **Bible** and the **Beads**. The resplendent seated figure, Mary Magdalen, ponders the sacred text. The figure standing beside her holds a highly ornate early form of the beads. It is the coupling of these two elements that gives the fullness of the Rosary.*

Cover design by Bill Bolger
Printed in the Republic of Ireland by Betaprint Ltd, Dublin

CONTENTS

1. There's Rhythm in the Rosary   5

2. There's Reason in the Rosary   8

3. There's Romance in the Rosary   11

4. The History of the Rosary   17

5. Beads are Beautiful   23

6. The Lord's Own Prayer   28

7. Rejoice, Mary   34

8. Full of Grace   37

9. The Lord is With You   41

10. Blessed Art Thou   44

11. Blessed is the Fruit…   48

12. Holy Mary, Mother of God   51

13. Holy Mary, Pray for Us   54

14. Us Sinners   57

15. Now and at the Hour of our Death   59

16. The Secrets of the Rosary   64

17. The Little Shared Prayer Group   68

18. The Healing Light of the Rosary   74

19. Meditation Made Easy   80

20. Mary Comes to Teach Us   87

21.	Dealing with Distractions	93
22.	Recent Popes Reflect on the Rosary	
	John XXIII	98
	Paul VI	100
	John Paul II	105
23.	The Ecumenical Bridges of the Beads	109
24.	Meditations	
	For personal and general use,	
	in private or with a group	117
	For the family	125
	Before Mass or in the presence	
	of the Blessed Sacrament	131

THERE'S RHYTHM IN THE ROSARY

'I can't take all that rhyming Hail Mary stuff.'

Wait a minute! Rhyme and rhythm can't be dismissed all that easily. It may be a natural enough reaction if you're just listening from outside. It's only when you get inside that you discover the secret of the Rosary.

Have you ever walked around a new housing estate and watched the building in progress? It's all a muddle of bricks and blocks and a din of noisy diggers and whirling cement mixers and houses half-finished. But come back months later and step inside. What was just a house, has become a home, with a young couple settling in to the rhythm and the romance of reasoned living. A house is made of sticks and stones, but only love and living can make a home.

So it is with the Rosary, until you make yourself at home with it. Only then do you find a soothing, healing rhythm which becomes a way of life. Music and dance, poetry and song – all these art forms have their rhythm and repetition. You may not always get the words of a song. They may be a jumble of sound, but the rhythm and the beat convey a whole world of meaning. Rhythm and rhyme form a basic and universal means of communication.

Life is full of rhythm. There is the rhythm of the seasons, of the winds and the waves. Sitting by the sea on a summer's day and listening to the lapping of the waters has soothed many a troubled mind and sore heart. Eating, drinking, resting and taking exercise are, of their very nature, rhythmic and repetitious. To disturb another's rhythm, whether that other be a human being, an animal or a plant, is to do violence to life.

So why complain about the rhyming of the Rosary? It is a

very good base from which to start. The fingering of the beads becomes a dance for the Lord and the murmur of the Our Fathers and Hail Marys becomes a song of the heart and music for the mind.

There will always be those who object to this rhythmic counting of beads, saying it is merely mechanical. The eminent Anglican priest Father Robert Llewelyn, in his delightful book *A Doorway to Silence,* published by Darton Longman & Todd, deals admirably with this by saying that 'there is a mechanical element in everything we do, for example in walking down the road. The totterings of a child indicate that the mechanics have not yet been grasped. Yet walking is not merely mechanical. We walk as people, not as zombies. The mechanical element in walking sets the mind free for holding conversation, admiring the scenery and so on. Similarly, in the saying of the Rosary, the mechanical element frees the mind to rest in the mysteries or, more simply, to find its repose in God. Pascal spoke of the use of the Rosary as the winning over of the machine, or the mechanical side of our nature, so that it helps instead of hindering the direction the spirit desires to take.'

The vocal rhythms

Something of this intriguing mechanics of prayer can be observed in the Lord's Prayer itself. It is full of harmony, of right order and perfect number:

Father

Thy Name – Thy kingdom – Thy will.

Father

Give us – Forgive us – Lead us – Deliver us.

The first three notes have an upward and outward swing, lifting the soul to the glory of God and the coming of his kingdom. This movement lifts us out of our selfish, earthbound ways. The second set of four notes brings us down to earth and reaches into the core of human need. As we praise God in the first half, we do so with uplifted hands. In the second half, we hold out our empty hands and, like little children, beg for bread and maybe jam or honey.

The Hail Mary has its own rhythm, which again is universal in its ability to commune with heaven and to communicate with others. The Hail Mary occurs one hundred and fifty times throughout the fifteen decades. This is to match the one hundred and fifty melodic Psalms. Like any song, it is repeated over and over again in a rhymed refrain, all for the purpose of delighting the heart and lifting the soul out of the mundane, into the world of the spirit. Only the unthinking and insensitive can knock this rhythm of the heavens.

Yes, indeed, the Hail Mary falls like a sound of the other world on this vale of tears. 'In the sixth month, God sent the angel Gabriel…'. We are talking about a given song, a heaven-sent sound. St Dominic heard a voice from heaven saying: 'Dominic, my son, be of good courage. Remember that the earth was dry and barren until watered by the dew of the heavenly Ave.'

Like the rhythm of the rain, the Hail Mary falls like liquid sunshine upon the barren land of our being. We simply expose ourselves to its downpouring upon the hardness of our hearts. There is a sense in which we do not so much say this prayer as listen to the Lord as he speaks to the maid of Nazareth and to the whole world whom she represented on that day of Annunciation. Reason will find its way, but the rhythm and rhyme will prepare a pathway. So, let's not despise the little earthy ways of the Rosary that lead to the heavenly highway.

THERE'S REASON IN THE ROSARY

The *Irish Rosary*, a magazine once produced by the Dominicans, had as its slogan: 'There's Reason in the Rosary!' To those who see the Rosary as a mere pious devotion, it might seem strange that such a devotion be committed by the Church to the Dominicans, an order of theologians and philosophers; and that popes and bishops down the centuries should ardently promote it.

But it is worth noting that there have been two streams of tradition which have gone into the making of the Rosary. There is the rhythm and the romance – 'the flowers of the fairest and blossoms the rarest' – and the crowning of Mary as Queen of the May. This is the popular piety stream which is treasured in the heart. But there is the other stream, the one that is governed by the reasoning mind.

The Dominican Order has as its principal mission the saving of souls through the preaching of the Gospel. The Rosary, in the hands of the Order of Preachers, as it is properly known, is a means towards that end. The famous French Dominican, Lacordaire, who enthralled the congregations of Paris with his teaching and his eloquence, spoke of the Rosary as 'the Gospel on its knees'. An older statement dating back to the 1500s describes the Rosary as 'more a method of preaching than of praying'.

The vocal prayers of the Rosary are either directly from the Scriptures or based on them. The mysteries are the preacher's handbook of the faith, containing all that he needs for proclaiming the Gospel. For those who know these mysteries, the beads become a pocket-book of Christian doctrine and equip them to give 'a reason for the faith that is in them'.

One of my own most precious memories is of sitting at the

feet of the great Dominican professor Garriogou Lagrange in the lecture halls of Rome, and later stumbling upon him during the holidays, walking up and down the sunny fields of his native France, swinging his Rosary beads like a child. And then there was Michael Cardinal Browne, the Irish Dominican who was one of the intellectual giants behind Vatican II. 'The Order', he would say, 'has two treasures of wisdom: The Summa Theologiae of St Thomas and the Rosary of St Dominic'. He told me how he loved the simplicity of the Rosary, and how he found in it all he needed for his spiritual nourishment, in the Our Father and the Hail Mary. The last time I saw him alive, he was pacing the front garden of the home of his brother Fr Maurice, where he whispered quietly: 'I'm saying the fifteen mysteries every day for the grace of a happy death.'

An instrument of evangelisation

Fr Vincent de Cousnongle, who headed the Dominican Order in the 1980s, showed his awareness of the rich doctrinal base of the Rosary when he wrote: 'Marian devotion has at times been accused of being more fervent than enlightened. However, we have moved from a view of the Rosary which is solely Mariological, to a Rosary that is Christological and centred on the Incarnation and the Paschal mystery. Here, Mary has her rightful place as servant of the Lord and spiritual mother of the disciples. We must not fear to accentuate this orientation... and make of the Rosary an organic presentation of the totality of the mystery of salvation. Is not this close to the plan of the primitive Dominican preaching? The Rosary can thus serve as framework for a real catechesis and primary evangelisation. Preachers of the Rosary are obliged to cultivate not only a humble, fervent, Marian piety, but also a serious biblical culture which must be kept up-to-date.'

This initial thrust of the Rosary as an instrument of evangelisation is evident from the original Privileged Votive Mass which was in use up to the Vatican II reform of the Missal. The Gospel of that text was taken from chapter eight of St Luke which begins 'Jesus journeyed through towns and villages, preaching and bringing the good news of the kingdom of God ... He said: "a sower went out to sow seed...".'

The text ends with the telling phrase 'To you it has been given to know the mysteries of the kingdom...'.

One might have expected the Gospel passage about the Angel announcing to Mary, as is to be found in the modern version of the Mass for 7 October. It would seem as if the original teaching-preaching passage got lost on the way. The original text well justifies the title of this chapter: 'There's reason in the Rosary.'

I kiss the wounds of your sacred head
with sorrow deep and true,
that each thought in my head today
be a million acts of love for you.

I kiss the wounds of your sacred hands
with sorrow deep and true,
that each touch of my hands today
be a million acts of love for you.

I kiss the wounds of your sacred heart
with sorrow deep and true,
that each beat of my heart today
be a million acts of love for you.

I kiss the wounds of your sacred feet
with sorrow deep and true
that each step I take today
be a million acts of love for you.

Something to hold on to

It was one of those nights in the Battle of Britain, with bombs
and incendiaries falling all over London. Maisie Ward was on
duty when a young man with ghastly wounds was carried into
the hospital. There was nothing medical she could do for the
man whose life was ebbing away.

As much to allay her own panic as to offer spiritual
assistance to the patient, she took out her beads and began to
pray: 'Holy Mary, Mother of God, pray for us sinners, now
and at the hour of our death.'

The man's eyes followed the woman's pale fingers and, slowly, painfully, he stretched out his hand and clasped the beads:

'Nurse', he moaned. 'It's something to hold on to.'

That's as good a way as any to be introduced to the Rosary. it is a lifeline; something to hold on to.

Personally, I'd think there was something missing if I couldn't find my beads to hand. I'd simply feel out of touch. But with the holy names of Jesus and Mary continually on my lips, and with the power of those mysteries of the Divine Humanity in the Rosary flowing through me, I know everything is all right. I take up the crucifix and kiss the Sacred Wounds of my Saviour.

It is sound psychology; I'm in touch with the people who matter. The beads are a kind of 'little sacrament' of the presence and the power of God.

Because I'm fully human, I like to have something to hold on to in my prayer life. A Rosary beads suits the purpose fine! Don't misunderstand me; there's nothing magical or mystical in the beads. It's just that I'm a total whole kind of human being; not a disembodied spirit, when I turn to God.

I once attended a weekend seminar on the Rosary conducted by a learned and holy priest. He had many beautiful things to say, but I've long since forgotten his wise words. What I do remember is how at the commencement of each talk, he picked up the crucifix and kissed it with love and reverence. For this man, the Rosary was no ritual round of the beads, but a whole romance with the person of Jesus. It wasn't a matter of saying prayers, so much as a way of relating in love to the one who was Lord of his life. Without this commitment to Jesus in faith, hope and love, spiritual exercises of any kind have little meaning.

My own reason for praying the Rosary is that it is a simple, yet supremely effective way of keeping in touch with the Lord. The mysteries of the Rosary reveal the secrets of his heart. His heart and mine become one, and in that single heart I love and move and have my being. Even when the mind is distracted, the heart can be right, as the will of the lover is fixed on the beloved. I cherish the lines of Sir Philip Sidney which echo this same truth:

> My true love hath my heart and I have his.
> By just exchange one for another given;
> I hold his dear, and mine he cannot miss,
> There never was a better bargain driven.
> My true love hath my heart and I have his.
>
> His heart in me keeps him and me in one,
> My heart in him, his thoughts and senses guides,
> He loves my heart, for once it was his own,
> I cherish his, because in me it bides.
> My true love hath my heart and I have his.

Many of the saints would have entered into the mysteries of Christ in this heart-fashion, conscious of the mystical marriage which took place in their lives. Jesus appeared to Catherine of Siena, and it seemed as if he had taken her heart away. She felt empty and bereft until Jesus returned later with his own heart in exchange. Something of this kind happens as we yield ourselves to the secret splendour of the Rosary mysteries. They are his mysteries, but they become ours. 'All we, beholding his glory, are being transformed into his likeness from one degree of glory to another', as Paul explains to the Corinthians.

The rhythm of Christ's life, death and glory which forms the golden thread of the Rosary, weaves itself into the pattern of our own lives. For those who regularly pray the fifteen mysteries, a secret cycle of loving identification develops. Christ's life flows into ours. Our joys and our sorrows are mingled with the water flowing from his side, and while our feet remain firmly on the earth, a longing for the glory of heaven fills out all our days. The beads become the companion of our souls.

Go to your heart-room

On a visit to Cloone House, in Poleglass, West Belfast, I met two young women leading a large group of children in deep, contemplative prayer – and I really mean that. The wonderful thing is that while it was as deep as the ocean and as high as the sky, it was all blissfully simple and entrancingly lovely.

They began with some happy singing and movement, with the two leaders, oblivious of my status as onlooking guest, just wrapped in their own prayerful concentration. A period of silence followed, and then two of the most beautifully recited decades of the Rosary I've ever shared. Each child said a Hail Mary slowly. They had been taught to rest in the Holy Name of Jesus and not rush in with the Holy Mary. They had been told that Jesus and Mary were present with them in the room. But, above all, these little ones had been instructed in the ways of meditation or, dare I say it, in the depths of Christian contemplation. They were told the story of the sacred event. But then they were taught to close their eyes, to sit very still, and go to their 'heart-room'. There, in that secret place, they would rest and look into the face of the Baby Jesus, and speak softly to his Mother.

During this time of stillness the two little ones on either side of me leaned their heads on my shoulder and almost fell asleep. I could only think of the words of Psalm 130:

> Truly I have set my soul
> in silence and peace.
> As a child has rest in its
> mother's arms.

These children were learning the secret of the Rosary, which is not so much a fixed and measured prayer, as a simple and effective way of finding Jesus in the midst of our own being.

We are not in the business of counting heads: how many come to our meeting, how many Rosaries we say, or get others to say. That has its place, but it is not the heart of the matter. As we practise what Pope Paul VI called the 'lingering rhythm of the Rosary' we learn to still our souls, and find our own 'heart-room'.

The history of my heart
Little wonder that Fr Abram J. Ryan could write in his poem, 'My Beads':

> Sweet blessed beads! I would not part
> With one of you for richest diadem;
> Ye know the history of my heart.
>
> For I have told you every grief
> In all the days of seventy years,
> And in your decades found relief.
>
> Ah! time has fled and friends have failed
> And joys have died; but in my needs
> Ye were my friends; my blessed beads!
> And ye consoled me when I wailed.

For many and many a time, in grief,
My weary fingers wandered round
Thy circled chain, and always found
In some Hail Mary, sweet relief.

How many a story you might tell
Of inner life, to all unknown;
I trusted you and you alone,
But ah! ye kept my secret well.

Ye are the only chain I wear
A sign that I am but the slave,
In life, in death, beyond the grave,
Of Jesus and His Mother fair.

The Rosary has its long natural history which can easily be told, but the history of the soul, and the secrets of the heart which go with it, can be charted only in the depths of being.

THE HISTORY OF THE ROSARY

Legend has it that at a time of great devastation in the early days of the thirteenth century, Our Lady came to St Dominic with the healing remedy of the Rosary. Scientific history may not have the kind of evidence to back up the tradition, but that matters little. The real question to be asked is not if this is true, but rather: What truth lies behind the legend? Indeed therein, lies a fascinating story.

I stumbled upon it many years ago, travelling through the South of France in the steps of St Dominic. It presented itself in quaint and crude form on one of those simple wooden plaques to be hung on a kitchen wall. It read:

> Three things that rule and ruin a man:
> Wine, Women and Wealth.

How horrible, you might say. It was an expression of that sour cynical thinking in that part of Europe at the time. It was a relic of the Manichaean heresy which had bedevilled Christianity in earlier centuries. The Catharist philosophy, as it was called, could be expressed summarily as follows: that while the spirit in human nature came from God, everything of the flesh and everything of the material creation was of some dark evil principle – call it the devil, if you like.

For the Catharists, a Greek term which means puritans, woman in particular came under attack, because she was the one who gave flesh to the pure soul. Even after death, her soul would not be allowed entry to heaven. She had to undergo a masculine reincarnation before that could happen. Childbirth was scorned and female children were often abandoned. To add insult to injury, this perverse understanding of woman could swing from the one extreme of excessive puritanism to the other, where woman, being of such slight import, could be indecently treated and abused.

Above all, the birth of Christ and the very notion of God becoming flesh and being born of woman was laughed at. It was expressed thus: Mary is not the mother of God; she is the vessel of flesh in which Jesus was shadowed forth. Sacraments which used earthly things like bread and wine, and water and oil were despised, and the Eucharist, in particular, was an abomination.

For the Catharists everything material for the maintenance of human life was scorned. Fasting unto death in order to set the spirit free of the prison house of the flesh was presented as an ideal. Hence the notion that wine, the usual drink of that region, and wealth that sustained life, were seen as the ruination of man. With this radical debasement of the physical creation, human sexuality was robbed of its divine dimension. Disordered and dichotomised humanity was split down the middle and cut off from its other half. To this warfare within the person was added war on the battlefield which led to plunder and pillage, and this in the name of God.

It was into this awful darkness that God shone a light in the persons of Francis and Dominic. St Francis preached the goodness of creation and raised a song of praise to the Creator of Brother Sun and Sister Moon; he became the patron of environmental and green movements down to our own day. St Dominic, inspired by the Queen of heaven, saw that the confusion and chaos sprang from one cause, the denial of the incarnation.

For if the Word, the second person of the Blessed Trinity had not disdained the Virgin's womb, but had truly taken flesh, then all flesh was holy. If the Son of God had assumed human nature, then all humanity has somehow been assumed by way of participation in the divine nature of Christ. And if men could gaze on Mary, the New Woman, 'our tainted nature's solitary boast', then they would view all women in the glory God had given them in the new creation. Here we find the emerging nucleus of the Rosary mysteries, built round the God who took flesh in the womb of Mary.

History and legend fall into line in the 'Go preach my Rosary' command to Dominic. Tradition has it that the Mother of God appeared to him in the forest of Bouconne, near Toulouse, in the midst of his crusade against the Catharists and addressed him thus:

> Wonder not, that until now, your labours have had such little fruit. You have spent them on a barren soil, not yet watered by the dew of divine grace. When God willed to renew the face of the earth, he began by sending down the fertilising dew of the Angelic Salutation. Go – preach my Rosary composed of one hundred and fifty Hail Marys, and you will obtain an abundant harvest.

The dry, barren earth lying under the original curse of Adam's fall was first brought back to life when that dew of the heavenly Ave first fell on Mary of Nazareth, 'the sweet benediction in the eternal curse', as one of the English poets expressed it. Another poet put it like this:

> He came all so still where his mother was,
> As dew in April that falleth on the grass.

What we do in the Rosary is to be still ourselves, like the patient, waiting grass, and allow the healing, fruitful blessing to fall upon us. There is a sense in which it is always Advent, as we wait in patient expectation, singing: 'Drop down dew, ye heavens, from above, and let the clouds rain the Just One.' For in the Hail Mary it is God who is speaking, first to Mary and then to all people who stand where she stood, allowing the golden rain of the Ave to fall on the desert of their being.

Slow evolution

Alongside that philosophic background to the Rosary in the days of St Dominic, must be considered the slow evolution of this prayer. As Eithne Wilkins in her delightful book, *The Rose Garden Game,* remarks: 'The Rosary was not suddenly invented or introduced, as rabbits were into Australia! It is more the story of a continuously evolving and living experience.'

This can be observed in paintings and mosaics of the twelfth century all over Europe and elsewhere. One deserving of special attention is to be found in the National Gallery in London, and is known as *The Betrothal of the Arnolfini.* Few of the thousands who stand before it each year, would be aware of its witness to the development of the Rosary. The work is by the Flemish painter, Jan Van Eyck, who died in 1441. For our purposes the date that matters is the one appearing over the convex mirror with the inscription: *Johannes de eyck fuit hic:* 1434 – Jan Van Eyck was present here: 1434.

Reflected in the mirror are two figures, very likely Van Eyck and his assistant, in addition to the couple themselves. Arnolfini and his bride stand in stately fashion in the centre, clasping hands as a symbol of consent. Above them is a single lighted candle, symbol of the divine presence A small dog represents the fidelity of marriage. There is a figurine, probably that of St Margaret of Antioch, patron of expectant mothers. Art critics have noted that the woman is not pregnant, as might appear. This is a pose and a dress style often given by Van Eyck to noblewomen, and indeed to angels, with their feminine, flowing garments.

Hanging on the wall to the left of the mirror, is a very definite and highly ornate Rosary, one of the earliest records we have of the high level of acceptance given to this devotion. By gracing the wall of such a distinguished merchant, it would appear that the Rosary was already taken for granted as normal Christian practice.

The highly stylised string of beads is much shorter than the five-decade beads in use today. The mirror frame itself depicts the mysteries, more or less as we know them today, but instead of fifteen, only ten are shown. It took another hundred years before the full depiction of fifteen mysteries began to appear. This is clear evidence of the evolutionary development of the Rosary. Indeed, there was a stage in the sixteenth century when the drawings in the famous editions of Andrea Gallerani, showed one hundred and fifty mysteries, one for each Hail Mary!

A practical point emerges from this survey, namely that while the present form of the Rosary was fixed by the Dominican Pope, Pius V, it need not be taken for granted that the form of this devotional practice is cut forever in tablets of stone. In recent years suggestions have been made about adding new mysteries, for instance: the Baptism of Christ, the Wedding Feast of Cana, or the Transfiguration. International congresses have frequently raised the matter. But the admonition has been given that the original structure, built around the Paschal cycle of life, death and glory, should be maintained.

As much a method of preaching as of praying!

The history of the Rosary embraces not only the structure of beads and decades, the number of mysteries and the nature of prayers, but concerns itself also with the purpose served by the Rosary through the centuries. In particular it must be noted that as well as being a prayer-form, the Rosary was used by the Dominicans as a method of teaching. It formed a kind of syllabus of the faith. One has always to ask why such a seemingly simple prayer should have been committed to the Order of Preachers. Pope Pius XI threw down this challenge to the Dominicans of 1934: 'The Rosary is, as it were, the principle and foundation on which the Order of St Dominic rests for perfecting the lives of its members, and obtaining the salvation of others.'

High sentiments those, yet they were fully accepted, it would seem, in the sixteenth and seventeenth centuries, which might be called the Golden Age of the Rosary. A visitor to Rome or Florence or to the National Library in Paris can feast on a whole range of Rosary literature which graphically points to the fact that the Rosary was indeed a powerful method of preaching as well as of praying. There are collections of sermons for the whole year as well as for the festivals, which incorporate the Rosary prayers and mysteries. It would seem as if the Rosary were not just one topic but rather a method of presenting the complete range of the faith. Miracles and healings on a vast scale are recounted in some of these priceless old volumes.

Over and above the evidence of the printed word, the art galleries of the world hold treasures of mosaic, sculpture and painting which show the place of the Rosary and the beads in Christian life. Anyone wishing to do a serious study of this vast and varied store would be greatly helped by the American Index of Art now housed in the Vatican Library. However, a note of warning. When you get your hands on this large volume, don't look under B for beads or R for Rosary. This is a high-tech index. Look under utensil!

BEADS ARE BEAUTIFUL

At Lourdes, Bernadette was fascinated by the beautiful string of beads which fell from Our Lady's arm. She observed that they were golden yellow, the same colour as the rose on each foot, and that 'the Lady slipped them through her fingers'. To show the importance of the physical beads themselves, the Lady once asked the child why she was not using her own Rosary but one lent to her by someone else for the occasion.

Beads are beautiful. They are Mary's own jewellery which she likes to share with us. And the amazing thing is that they are catholic in the widest sense of that word. For Bernadette, they were a golden chain linking heaven to earth, but research shows that they are also a silver thread binding many cultures together.

For the Rosary has not only a history, but also a geographical and cultural spread. It is to be found in some form or other among Hindus, Buddhists, Muslims and Jews. Some would suggest that wherever you see a Rosary, there you find a Roman Catholic, while many sincere Protestants have a holy fear of the beads which they class as 'Papist superstition.'

All this is far from the truth. The very term 'rosary' is in no way exclusive to Catholics. The fact is, that neither the restricted Roman Catholic view nor the Protestant objection hold water. The fingering of beads and the accompanying meditation, together with the very name, Rosary, are part of the spiritual patrimony of the world. So true is this, that it can be said without fear of contradiction, that to abandon or destroy the practice of the Rosary, would be an act of sheer vandalism, a kind of spiritual genocide.

Part of nature and of history

Pascal spoke of the beads as 'part of the whole philosophy of the Church about man's nature.' One can go further. They are part of the world's philosophy!

Pascal continues: 'We are not pure spirit but composite beings made of spirit and matter. And so we need, if our prayer is to be true to our nature, to use material things: images either set before our eyes or fashioned in the imagination, the cross at the end of our beads, the blessing that makes them sacred, the prayers we say on them. The world around us is one huge distraction from prayer. The very holding, the very slipping through our fingers of the beads, can be a powerful counter-distraction.'

Pious Hindus use the beads to keep count of invocations to their gods, but also as a means of promoting contemplation. Much store is put on the beads themselves, and some can be obtained only from an accomplished Yogi. There is an account of one old hermit exerting great physical energy in turning a large wheel with huge beads attached. The Rosary plays a part in the initiation of children to the cult of Vishnu, and there are collections of invocations used on such occasions, such as: 'Homage to the adorable Rama.' These invocations are repeated over and over, and are known as 'mantras'. They are meant to still the wandering mind and induce harmony and healing.

In Tibet, the word for telling the beads means literally 'to purr like a cat'. Contemplatives have always been attracted by the rhythmic hum of purring cats and have often adopted them as companions. One Irish monk kept his Pangur Ban (white Pangur cat) in his cold monastic cell to keep him alert in his meditation and study. Personally, I love to say the Rosary, with a certain Black Beauty as a crooning comfort purring away on my lap. Her soothing vibrations make a rhythmic hum to accompany the murmur of the Hail Marys, as well as keeping me in tune with God's creation. (Not a bad idea for one who refuses to go Catharist!)

In Persia and India, the Rosary is called 'tasbih', deriving from the Arabic word meaning to praise, or to exalt. The Prophet Mohammed attributed great merit to reciting the names of God and giving praise to Allah a hundred times in the morning and again in the evening.

From Egypt comes a record of wakes for the dead with continuous recitation of Rosaries, punctuated with strong coffee. At certain stages, the prayer-leader asks aloud: 'Have ye transferred the merit of your prayers to the soul of the deceased?' The reply is: 'We have so transferred them, praised be God, the Lord of all creatures.' Reminiscent of the Rosary at an Irish wake!

In Greek monasteries, just as in so many Roman Catholic institutions, a knotted cord or string of beads is used as part of the religious garb. The laity use a smaller cord which is known as 'worry beads' to settle the frayed nerves and induce a restful and contemplative mind. They are treasured as a means to prayer and peace of mind.

Worry beads
Tension, they say, passes out through the extremities of the body. There is something basically human about touching and holding the beads. A glossy society magazine some time ago, showed the actress Sophia Loren with a 'worry beads' in her hand, trying to keep cool as she watched her favourite football team in action. The proper Greek term for these beads, is 'kombologion' which indicates that a collection of holy invocations would be recited on them. The Russians use the word 'chotki' for this same form of Rosary. Some suggest that many of these eastern prayer-forms were picked up by the Crusaders, on their way to and from the Holy Land, and so

found their way into Europe. Of this, we just can't be certain. In any event, they seem to be basic and universal human practices.

Influence of the Irish

In the fifth century St Patrick recited one hundred Our Fathers during the long nights on the mountain as he guarded his master's sheep. Irish monks who followed him would recite one hundred and fifty Paters, based on the same number of the biblical Psalms. They must have provided themselves with some simple counting device, perhaps a string of stones or wild berries. The Paters were frequently recited in three sections, which gave rise to the expression 'na trí caocait' (the three fifties.) It has been suggested, that this was a forerunner of the Rosary, with its triple division into Joyful, Sorrowful and Glorious mysteries. Again, because of the association with the Psalms, the earliest title by which the Rosary was known in the Gaelic language was Saltair Mhuire (Psalter of Mary.) Strangely enough, the word 'Rosary', common to so many languages, does not exist in the Irish language. Quite likely, the Irish would have been influenced by the reform of the Dominican Order at the time of Alan de la Roche who himself disliked the word Rosary. 'It smacked', he said, of 'profanity betokening the vain and florid practices of putting crowns of roses on young ladies.' He advocated instead the biblically associated title of Psalter of Mary.

We have no record of a fixed number of decades in the days of St Dominic, but simply an account of how the saint would preach for a certain length of time and then invite his listeners to pick up the beads and ponder the teaching he had shared with them. This rudimentary exercise provided the nucleus for a future form of the Rosary. It was not until the pontificate of Pius V at the time of the Battle of Lepanto (October 1571), that the Rosary took on its present shape.

The Irish Folklore Commission has made a collection of rich prayers that accompanied the recitation of the Rosary, and Irish museums, like other galleries throughout Europe, display a variety of Rosary beads used over the centuries. Highly ornate beads were often handed down as family heirlooms. For those who might be put off by five or fifteen decades all at once there are some beautiful specimens of single decade beads and Rosary rings, all part of our Irish heritage. Factory-made modern versions of these abound, including the lovely Connemara Marble Paidrín Beag (Little Prayer Beads).

THE LORD'S OWN PRAYER

An old writer asked 'Why do we say ten Hail Marys and only one Our Father to each decade of the Rosary?' The answer was: The Our Father is the foundation prayer and we lay only one foundation. When building a house we pile up bricks and blocks and mountains of cement and plaster and wood and tiles and lay them on the foundation. So it is with the Lord's Prayer. It is the basis for our spiritual home.

Master, teach us to pray

The Gospel describes how Jesus was in a certain place praying, when the apostles came to him and said: 'Master, teach us to pray, as John also taught his disciples to pray.' If only we would take that request to heart and make it our own, it would be enough. Night and day, in the church before the Blessed Sacrament, on the roads and in the workplace, sitting, standing or sleeping, that plea should be in the depths of our being and become our longing desire: 'Master teach us to pray...'.

I'm reminded of my parents whose own faith became my first call to prayer. As a boy, I observed them at prayer, and such was the impression they made on my wild young mind that it has lived with me to this day. They would call me to join them for the Rosary each night. We said it before the image of the Sacred Heart, and in the glow of the red sanctuary lamp I could see their intent faces with eyes towards the face of the Christ. Their gaze seemed to reach beyond the small statue and the bedroom walls to an invisible world which was more precious and more important to them than the material space where we lived out our earthly existence.

Like many young folk, my faith at the time was pretty weak. I wasn't sure if there was a God at all, or if there was anything beyond this world of sight and sound. But this I could see. My Dad, a down-to-earth man, who knew the difference between a penny and a pound, saw something, and I knew you couldn't cod John Joe Harty. And my wise mother, a primary school teacher, stood for no nonsense and gave her children a sense of responsibility. Her faith and love of God glowed more brightly than the red light burning before the Sacred Heart lamp which she burned night and day. Something of that light lives with me still.

They had faith. Not that they taught us. We simply caught it from the pair of them. They were in touch with the heavenly Father and with the Mother of us all. Because of their faith, I began to grasp that there was a God who knows and who listens to the sighs of humanity. My parents did not have much to leave me in the way of material goods, but they left me a faith in God my Father, a faith that has been the foundation for everything else.

In the same way the apostles observed Jesus and knew that he was in touch with a great someone who reigned above, yet was intimately concerned and close at hand. In Jesus, heaven and earth were linked up, in a manner more amazing than any modern satellite link-up. No wonder they wanted in on the secret and cried: 'Master, teach us…'.

The mind of the Master

And what teaching there is in this prayer! It lets us into the mind of the Master. We call it the Lord's Prayer, not only because he taught it, but also because it reflects his own personal prayer in certain ways. It helps us to think his thoughts and to feel with his heart. The prayer contains everything we need to ask for and in the proper order of asking. It shows us how to seek first the kingdom of God, and only then, the things we need for everyday earthly living. It puts a priority on the praise of God and the accomplishment of his sovereign will. It lets the cares of the body and the concerns of bread and butter fall naturally into their own place.

How often we get worried and anxious rushing in with our material petitions, and then wonder why things don't work out. We need to get back to the Lord's own prayer, which begins with praise of God, our Father: '*thy* name, *thy* kingdom, *thy* will'. That should be the set of a soul seeking the divine assistance. Jesus is so clear: 'I tell you, do not worry about your life, what you will eat or drink, or about your body, what you will wear. Look at the birds of the air; they do not sow or reap or store away in barns, and yet your heavenly Father feeds them.'

The robin and the sparrow

There is a poem about a robin wondering why the human beings rush about and worry so. The sparrow gives the quirky answer: 'It must be that they have no heavenly Father, such as looks after you and me!'

Jesus says: 'You are much more valuable than they.' We have to be as carefree as the sparrow. But that kind of freedom happens only when we become soaked in the praise of our Father and have made his honour our prime purpose. We come to understand that he will never be outdone in honouring our wishes. With God, it is a case of *noblesse oblige* – nobility imposes obligations! The order in the Lord's Prayer helps us understand how God stands in relation to us, and how we in turn should stand in his presence.

It reminds me of Joe, an easygoing fellow, who lived for his football, for his success in life, his drink with the lads and generally for his own single self. His philosophy might be summed up in the words: 'What's in it for me?' But when he fell in love, got married and had a child, Joe changed overnight. I met him in the house holding his new-born son in his arms, with that glow in his eyes that fathers have for a first-born child. 'It changes your priorities. I know now, who I really am, and I hope my little one grows up to be proud of my name', is all Joe could say.

And that's how God is with us and we are with him. As we learn first to praise his holy name, we then slip quietly and confidently into the way of opening our hands to say: 'Give us, forgive us, lead us, deliver us'. Our God is no single solitary, no lone ranger in the sky. He is a family person at home with his Son and with the brooding mother Spirit as he holds each one of us in the hollow of his hand.

Through him, with him, in him

When we say 'Our Father', it is not just that we are joined with others and share a common father with them. Over and above that union, we say 'our' because we are one with Christ himself. We are privileged to be his brothers and sisters, through him, with him, and in him, addressing the one Father. This is what gives effectiveness to our prayer. When we cry 'Abba, Father' it is the voice of his own beloved Son that the Father hears and cannot refuse. Our prayer has become the Lord's Prayer.

It is sometimes said, that what matters in the Rosary is not the vocal prayers, but the contemplation of the mysteries, which are its heart and soul. I find that a disturbing and misleading statement. In the first instance no prayer can be merely vocal. Otherwise, it would fall under Jesus' condemnation of babbling, vain words. There must be an element of meaning and loving attention present at all times. The Lord's Prayer is not only the foundation, it is also the summit of prayer, the prayer that gives us the mind of Christ and lifts us to the heavenly places. 'Let this mind be in you which was also in Christ Jesus,' says St Paul. The purpose of the mysteries is to fill us with this mind and give direction to our desire, so enabling us to ask effectively in the name of Jesus.

In my name

This is always my concern when people come hungry with desire for this and that intention. I like to cry out in Jesus' name: 'If you ask the Father anything in my name, he will give it to you. Hitherto, you have not asked anything in my name. Ask and you will receive.'

Just think about what that means, *asking in my name;* surely there is the heart of the matter. The conditions have to be right for reception of the divine favours, as, I often observed with the boys at St Gerard's boarding school in Bray. They would be lined up before dinner when Mr Murphy would ask them all to stretch out their hands for examination before going into the dining room. Anyone with dirty fingers and black nails was sent back to the washroom with the the headmaster's words ringing in their ears: 'Look at those hands, you're in no fit condition to sit at table'. Before sitting at God's table and partaking of his gifts, we must get ourselves into the right condition to receive.

Jesus has made it so clear. 'You have not asked in my name. Ask in my name, and the Father will respond.' That's not simply a question of saying the name with our lips. It means being of one mind with Jesus, letting those words of his penetrate our whole being: 'His name is as ointment poured forth.' Those first words of the Lord's Prayer, 'thy name', 'thy kingdom', 'thy will', must become the set of our souls. Surrendering to the divine plan we submit to the bitter-sweet process of allowing the mysteries of Christ's life, death and glory take over our lives. 'In him we live and move and have our being.'

Only then can we hold out clean hands and ask for daily bread. Only then, with clean hearts, can we truly reach out hands to receive. Only then can we find the grace to forgive and forget and be delivered from evil.

St Thomas Aquinas puts it thus: 'The Lord's Prayer is the most perfect of prayers. In it, we ask, not only for all the things we can rightly desire, but also in the proper order that they should be desired. The splendid final section in the Catechism of the Catholic Church remarks that if we say the Lord's Prayer sincerely, this right order spreads right through our whole lives. 'We leave individualism behind, because the love that we receive frees us from it. The "our" at the beginning ... like the "us" of the last four petitions, excludes no one. If we are to say it truthfully, our divisions and oppositions have to be overcome.' (2792)

Rejoice, Mary

As part of an ecumenical gathering, I was asked to pray with someone who was ill. Because I believe strongly that Mary is the nurse of the wounded Lamb of God, I see her as having a real place in any Christian healing ministry, so I wanted to bring the Mother of God in somehow. I had a hunch however, that the woman who had asked was a staunch Protestant and not quite ready for a full-blooded Hail Mary. For that reason, I used the version: *Rejoice, O highly favoured One,* which occurs in many modern translations. The petitioner was thrilled and took it as a great word of healing. From there on, her depression lifted and she really rejoiced in the Lord. Anyway, that's what the Hail Mary is all about and it is for everyone who is called Christian.

All things new

The Angel Gabriel was clearly announcing the dawn of the new creation of rejoicing, not only for Mary for but all humanity. Where the word *Hail* is found in our popular prayer, the original Greek word has: *Rejoice.* It is the fulfilment of the prophetic word: 'Look, I am going to create new heavens and a new earth, and the past will not be remembered and will come no more to mind. Rather be joyful, for look, I am creating Jerusalem to be *Joy* and my people to be *Gladness'* (Isaiah 65:17-18).

We're often tempted to think that religion is a matter of *pull down the shutters and let's all be sad.* The truth is the very opposite. The Christian message is one of opening up to joy. The word that Mary heard from heaven was: 'Rejoice, O highly favoured one'.

Those who say their prayers in Irish will know that instead

of 'Hail' we have a rich expression which might be translated: 'Praise and blessing to you, Mary', or, as another Irish working has it: 'The fullness of life and joy to you'. And this is no ordinary joy. It is the opening up of a whole landscape of salvation history and fulfilment of prophecy.

The Daughter of Zion spoken of in the book of Zephaniah (3:14-18) is now actualised in the person of Mary the Virgin of Nazareth. She is no isolated individual but stands out as the representative of humanity. When the Angel of the Lord speaks to Mary, he speaks to everyone. The whole world is called to *Rejoice* in this Woman.

Little wonder that the Church puts before us in so many of the Marian Masses the splendid words of Zephaniah:

> Shout for joy, O daughter of Zion,
> Sing joyfully, O Israel!
> Be glad and rejoice with all your heart,
> O daughter of Jerusalem!
> The King of Israel, the Lord is in your midst,
> a mighty saviour.
> He will rejoice over you with gladness
> and renew you in his love.

The God who 'creates in Jerusalem a joy' is still doing so, and still 'singing over each one of us, as on festivals' (Zephaniah 3).

Messianic greeting is for all

The greeting on Gabriel's lips is no banal salute but has to be understood in the well-grounded biblical history of the blessings to be poured out on humanity in the Messianic times. The wonderful thing is, that as we enter into God's rejoicing over his choicest creature, the joy spills over on ourselves. For this is not just our simple prayer addressed to the Virgin Mary. It is God's own proclamation of the Good News. It is our Father in heaven who is taking the initiative, pouring out his joy on all humanity. Mary was our representative on the first day of Annunciation. I say 'first' day because annunciation is an ongoing reality. Divine favour and rejoicing is a flood of mighty waters flowing from the bosom of the Trinity and we are all caught up in it. The key that opens the floodgates for us is surely the same angelic salutation as at the Annunciation to Mary.

FULL OF GRACE

Gabriel did not call the virgin of Nazareth by her personal name, Mary, but rather by the splendid title, 'full of grace', usually translated in modern versions as 'highly-favoured One'.

One might be misled by the English text, 'favoured', as if we were talking about something past and finished with. The Greek has a twofold past tense unknown to English grammar: the aorist, which is a kind of a full-stop past, and the perfect, which is the one used here, and which implies, not only a past condition, but an ongoing reality as if to say: 'Rejoice, you who have been, and still are being favoured…'.

No need, however, to give up on the well-established 'full of grace' expression, which we have in the familiar form of the Hail Mary. It conveys an aspect of grace which is fundamental to Catholic thinking. For some, the phrase 'highly favoured' might seem to stop at some kind of external regard, and not penetrate to the core of the being as grace does.

What do we mean when we say that Mary is *full* of grace? We do not mean that she is *full* in the way that a glass is full of water. The water is simply there, in place inside the glass. It does nothing to the glass itself. It relates to the glass in a merely static, extrinsic way.

Something far more beautiful

Divine grace in Mary, or indeed in any of us, operates in a far higher and more beautiful manner than that. It has an intrinsic and life-giving relationship with the human personality.

Look for a moment at a *rose* within the glass. The water is doing something for that rose that is way beyond anything it does for the glass. It is causing the rose to live and to bloom in all its loveliness. The rose is not just *placed* in the water. All the life-giving chemical elements of the water are being conveyed to the rose, so that there is a *vital* union between the two.

The water is *in* the glass.

The rose is *watered.*

There is a world of difference between those two situations. Instead of a mere static physical presence, the rose enjoys an ongoing, living relationship of dependence on the water. While no mere image can convey the mystery of divine grace, we have here a faith picture of the wonderful world of the supernatural which fills and floods the personality of Mary, the mother of Jesus.

Mary is not just *full* of grace; she is always being *filled* with this transforming gift. She is *full* of grace, in the sense that she is forever being filled to the full capacity of a creature with the overflowing abundance that streams forth in a river of life from the heights of the Most Blessed Trinity. Daughter of the Father, mother of the Son and bride of the Holy Spirit, she is queen of all creation, and the instrument through which grace is poured out on all humanity.

What do we mean by *grace?*

What then is the meaning of this grace for which Mary is singled out for a special fullness? The term is so rich in meaning, that scholars have spent their lives discussing it. It embraces the whole of God's goodness, the sacred humanity of Jesus, the riches of the sacraments and all the treasury of the Church poured forth upon humanity. Grace-filled humanity is no longer a fallen sin-filled creature, no longer a mere servant of the Creator, but a friend of God. Jesus spoke of this at the Last Supper when he told his disciples that he would no longer call them *servants* but *friends.*

The distinction between servant and friend has enormous

implications, which Jesus went on to explain. 'I shall not call you servants any more, because a servant does not know his master's business; I call you friends, because I have made known to you everything I have learnt from my Father' (John 15:14-16).

The servant in a house or workshop simply does what he's told. He gets on with the job. The friend, on the other hand, particularly the kind of close friend Jesus talks about here, enjoys an intimate relationship, which brings him into a close bond of union. So amazing is the bond of divine grace that St Peter writes of it as bringing us to 'share the divine nature' itself (2 Peter 1:4).

Grace then, is more than a gift handed over from an outside source, however sublime. Grace enters into the personality – touches the very being and transforms us into new creatures. There is a real sense in which it *divinises* our humanity. In no way does it do violence to humanity; rather it enhances and perfects it.

Neither must we think in terms of being half human, half divine, or that we become less human as we make progress in the ways of grace. The glorious truth of being *full of grace* is that we are called to be one hundred per cent human, one hundred per cent divine. Fully graced people, as Mary is, are delightfully human and normal. Saints are in no danger of becoming mermaids, half one thing, half the other, neither fish nor flesh, so heavenly-minded as to be no earthly good.

Christians live well in both worlds

There is something healthily holy and wholesome about Christianity. It is about the Word that became flesh and dwelt among us. Like Jesus, the divine humanity, Christian saints know how to live well in both worlds. That is the secret that Mary treasured in her heart from that first moment, when the

angel said to her: 'Hail full of grace, the Lord is with thee'.
Little wonder that when Bernadette saw Our Lady in the
grotto of Lourdes, she exclaimed: 'You would wish to die and
go to heaven to see her'.

Inspired by the ancient shrine of Our Lady of Graces at St
Mary's, Pope's Quay, Cork, I would like to end this section
with a prayer I composed many years ago.

To Our Lady of Graces
O Mary of every Grace
intercede for us,
that we may receive the outpouring
of God's love, as you did.

You were chosen by God
and received his blessing, in
those wondrous words:
'The Lord is with thee...'

Share, O Mary, that blessing with us
that we too may know
the power of those words:
'The Lord is with thee...'

Help us realise that we have nothing to fear
for the Lord is with us.
We are wise and strong and can do all things
in Christ, who strengthens us.

O Mary of all Graces, we greet you
as the Father, Son and Holy Spirit
greeted you:
'The Lord is with thee...'

Pray for us, O Holy Mother, now
and at the hour of our death. Amen.

THE LORD IS WITH YOU

Over in the West of Ireland, I was made welcome for a Rosary Novena by a wonderful woman who had organised the whole event. Each day we walked on the strand near Ballina while we prayed and talked things over. At the end, she said: 'I'll miss you when you're gone. Please write something in my memo book so that I'll remember this novena.' I thought of writing something lovely, like 'God gave us memory, so that we might have roses in December', but instead I settled for jotting down 'Nan, the Lord is with you.'

Nan looked disappointed. The words were so few, and seemingly so uninspiring. So I added to the little message: 'This is all our Lady knew, but it was enough. It is everything.'

The truth is, that these words, 'the Lord is with you' are covenant words. They are a summation of all God's promises throughout the sacred scriptures. These are the words God spoke to Joshua when he was frightened of leading the people of Israel into the Promised Land. It was feared that there were giants in the land and that the people would be devoured like grasshoppers before them. Not feeling up to the stature of the great Moses, Joshua needed to hear these words of the Lord:

> My servant Moses is dead. Every place that the sole of your foot will tread, I have given you, as I promised to Moses. As I was with Moses, so I will be with you. I will not fail you or forsake you. Be strong and courageous. Do not be frightened or dismayed, for the Lord your God is with you, wherever you go. (Joshua 1)

That is the very stuff of the covenant: I will be with you. You will never walk alone. Mary had to walk into an unknown land, an uncharted course. She had to walk in the darkness of faith. She had nothing but that word of the angel: 'the Lord is with you', and her only and total response was: 'Let that word be done to me'. That was Our Lady's 'yes' to this ultimate expression of God's covenant and she proclaimed it on behalf of all the people.

Dynamic presence – new relationship

This 'being with his people' is not a mere physical presence, like the way the chair is present in the room. What we are talking about is a living, dynamic presence, bringing about a whole new relationship. The Lord is with us, backing us up, sending us forth into our own personal land of promise, and pledging protection every step of the way. This is much more than a contract which stops short at an exchange of goods or services. Covenant touches the core of our being. When Jesus says 'This is the cup of my blood, the blood of the new and everlasting covenant', he is going beyond the conveyance of gifts and goods. He is offering his very self. 'This is my body given up for you. This is my blood shed for you. This is me handed over into your hands.'

This is the kind of offering that happens in marriage, where a man says to his bride: 'With this body, I thee worship.' He is placing his body, his life in the hands of his beloved. So the Lord himself is placing the body of his Son in the hands of humanity, thus bringing about a true covenant, a mystical marriage which begins in the wedding hall of Mary's womb.

The case of David and Jonathan illustrates the depths of relationship to which a genuine covenant can lead. The story begins with an exchange of goods and possessions. Jonathan takes off his royal cloak and gives it to David. He then hands over his princely sword and his girdle which would very likely have contained his purse. When David then ventured forth, he would be seen in the princely mantle, carrying the sword of authority, and with royal gold and silver to support himself. David would now be the weak one vested in the armour of the strong one, the poor one endowed with the riches of the great one. That is the essence of biblical covenant.

So much for the contract, the exchange of goods and gifts. But these were simply tokens; tokens pointing to the deeper reality which was the personal bond of friendship between Jonathan and David, sealed in a blood covenant. 'The soul of Jonathan was knit to the soul of David, and Jonathan loved him as his own soul. Whatever you say, I will do for you. And David said: Deal kindly with your servant for you have brought your servant into a sacred covenant with you...' (1 Samuel 19:8-10; 20:1-17)

God made many covenants with his people, pledging that come what may, come hell or high water as it were, he would not desert his own. 'Though all are mine, you will be my peculiar people, my special possession.' As the Eucharistic Prayer has it, 'Again and again God made a covenant with his people'. But now, in the fullness of time, the ultimate covenant is cut, that made in and through Mary, as heaven and earth are brought together in this sacred person-to-person marriage promise: The Lord is with you.

Little wonder that the Litany of Loreto calls Mary the Ark of the Covenant. In that Ark, we all find a home and know that the Lord is with us. There, we are all sealed in that precious blood of the Lamb which he drew from the veins of his mother. As we attune ourselves to those words proclaimed by the Angel Gabriel, the strong Immortal One reaches out to each one of us with those covenant terms: 'Do not be afraid. As I was with Moses, so I will be with you.'

BLESSED ART THOU

'Blessed art thou among women,
Blessed is the fruit of thy womb.'

The rhythm and the balance of this two-part statement are beautifully suited to the quiet contemplation of the Rosary mysteries. The statement brings Jesus and Mary together where they belong. And like the first section of the Ave, this piece is straight out of Holy Scripture. Far from being a mere pious ejaculation, this is a further proclamation of the Gospel. The words in St Luke are introduced in a most solemn manner: 'Elizabeth was filled with the Holy Spirit and cried in a loud voice.' The loud cry is the cry of the Holy Spirit. It is the same that Jesus gave in the moment of victory on the Cross: 'With a loud cry, he gave up the spirit.' No need, then, to apologise to anyone for our use of these words of Elizabeth. They are the fruit of the Holy Spirit.

We know too, that they are prophetic words, and are confirmed by Mary herself when, in her overshadowing by the Holy Spirit, she cries: 'Henceforth, all ages shall call me blessed.' Later in St Luke a woman shouts aloud: 'Blessed is the womb that bore you and the breasts that nursed you' (11:27-28). Jesus replies: 'Blessed rather, are they who hear the word of God and keep it.'

This is no put-down of Mary. Jesus is telling of the true greatness of his mother, declaring her a faithful disciple of the word. As for the evangelist Luke, he has already told us that Mary had replied to the angel: 'Let your word be done to me' (1:38). Again, 'Mary pondered these words in her heart' (2:19, 51).

With complete scriptural confidence then, and under the

inspiration of the Holy Spirit, we can say these further words which proclaim the blessedness of Mary. In the final analysis, it is the Lord himself we are praising for the favour he has poured out on his mother. This is one of the great secrets of prayer, that we go out of our own selfishness to rejoice in the goodness we find in another of God's creatures.

Two distinct rhythms in the Ave

Tradition wisely gives us the Ave Maria in two halves (the Hail Mary and the Holy Mary) for the recitation of the Rosary. The first half is more properly seen as a statement of the good news, a proclamation of the Gospel, and a song of joy, as we praise God for the mighty things he has done in Mary. It is eminently suitable as a refrain to our meditation on the mysteries of the divine humanity. The second part of the Holy Mary is our human response to the divine outpouring. It is necessary to observe this double rhythm if we are to pray the Rosary well.

As someone leads with the Hail Mary, we let ourselves be quiet and open to the divine blessing from above. As the Psalmist has it: 'I have stilled and quieted my soul, as a child has rest in its mother's arms.' Responding with the Holy Mary, we become active, joining with the whole people of God, as we seek the intercession of this woman for all seasons.

One can understand the difficulty some have in making a ritual exercise of proclaiming Mary blessed. They would prefer to emphasise the teaching of Ephesians (1:3,) where we read: 'Blessed be the God and Father of our Lord Jesus Christ, who has blessed us with all the spiritual blessings of heaven in Christ.' That indeed is the truth, but it in no way rules out the blessing that every creature has, by its incorporation into Christ. The fact that Jesus is King and sovereign Lord, does not mean that the creature is a mere puppet on a string. The glory of God is achieved when human beings are fully alive, graced in the beloved and contributing in their own way to the work of salvation.

Mary herself gives confirmation of this when she proclaims that: 'He that is mighty has done great things for me.' In saying this she does not deny her own blessedness. Neither must we. The Ecumenical Declaration of 1979 from Saragossa puts this well when it states: 'If we praise the saints, and in particular the Virgin Mary as the Mother of God, this praise is rendered essentially to the glory of God who, in glorifying the saints, crowns his own gifts.'

It is not to the saint or to Mary that we ultimately pay the honour but to the source of all blessing, who more than pays us back 'with all the spiritual blessings of heaven'.

Praise is no optional extra

Praise is no optional extra. It is a just debt, and it must be paid. Perhaps the way of petition comes more easily, but we build up a false confidence by not laying down a solid deposit of praise. Anyone who has read Merlin Carruther's extraordinary book, *From Prison to Praise,* will understand the miracle-power wonder of this practice. We learn to praise God for all his wonders, for his blessings poured out on others, and on ourselves. Above all, we learn to praise him for himself: 'hallowed be thy name.' The business world knows only too well that it pays to be hearty in your appreciation and lavish in your praise. In the realm of the spirit, it is a still more precious commodity, and it pays the highest dividends.

The Rosary, with its praise of Mary and of the blessed fruit of her womb, is an excellent down-payment, bringing with it the pledge and the promise of eternal reward. Rightly do we end each Rosary with the plea:

Pray for us, O holy Mother of God,
That we may be made worthy of the promises of Christ.

BLESSED IS THE FRUIT...

Speed kills! the road sign screams. So too with the highway of the Rosary. Speed destroys its rhythm and kills the spirit, and the principal victim is the Holy Name of Jesus. Once at a large gathering of priests and laity, the Rosary was being recited in common and I had brought a devout member of the Plymouth Brethren along. Half-way through she began to cry softly to herself, then got up and walked wearily out of the chapel. Following her, I asked: 'Lillian, why do you weep?'

'Because they have taken my Lord away', she replied, reminding me of the desolate cry of Mary of Magdala on the morning of the Resurrection, when she found the empty tomb. 'Why', asked my friend, 'must so many devout priests, and their flock, rob Jesus of his glory? They rush on through the Holy Mary and smother the name of Jesus.'

How true, and how many Rosaries rich in promise are robbed of their power and glory by failing to rest in the Holy Name. Before the leader is near the end of the first half of the Ave, the Holy Mary is rushed in. I believe that the Mother of God herself must weep as she sees her Son robbed of his glory. Far better might it be to say fewer decades and say them well, putting quality before quantity.

Over the years, I have introduced people to the Rosary by centering on the Holy Name, beginning very often with a song like 'His name is as ointment poured forth', singing it over and over again until a rhythm of peace and contemplation is established. I have encouraged people to sit back and relax, even to lie flat on the floor, breathing out all anxiety and worry and breathing in the healing that comes from the name of Jesus. I like to read the text from the Acts of the Apostles about the crippled man who sat begging at the gate called Beautiful and was cured in the name of Jesus.

> Peter said, 'Silver and gold I do not have, but what I have I give you. In the name of Jesus Christ of Nazareth, walk.' The cripple jumped to his feet and, walking and jumping and praising God, ran into the Temple courts; and all were filled with amazement. (Acts 3)

The practice of saying the Rosary before the Blessed Sacrament has brought about a delightful way of making this emphasis on the Holy Name a reality. It is recommended to make each Hail Mary a spiritual Communion with the Lord. When you come to the name of Jesus, offer him to the Eternal Father or, rather, offer yourself with him to the Father, so that your action becomes a little liturgy, a living out of the Mass. And conscious of the mystery you are contemplating, draw from that mystery the grace you need. Let the power which still goes out from Jesus touch and transform your life. Resting in him you are making a spiritual communion, with all the blessings that go with that practice.

The Jesus clauses
Elizabeth had already greeted Mary as 'blessed among women'. Under that same impulse of the Holy Spirit, she added: 'blessed is the fruit of your womb.'

It was the Church that later completed the phrase by inserting the name of Jesus. One of the methods used to make this practice more fruitful was the inclusion of the 'Jesus clauses' in the Rosary, a custom which consisted of adding to the name of Jesus a short reference to the mystery under consideration. One of the best examples comes from

Dominic of Prussia, but St Louis Marie de Montfort has a whole series of his own.

I give here a few examples of Jesus clauses which have been used in recent times:

The Annunciation:	Jesus, given to each one of us.
Presentation:	Jesus, revealing the thoughts of many.
Scourging:	Jesus, by whose wounds we are healed.
Crucifixion:	Jesus, pierced by a lance.
Descent of the	
Holy Spirit:	Jesus, pouring out the Spirit on all flesh
Coronation:	Jesus, who is Lord.

Of course this custom developed at a time when only the first half of the Hail Mary was in use, ending with the phrase: 'blessed is the fruit of your womb.' In the present arrangement, it has not been so helpful as it seems to hinder the flow of the Holy Mary. However, it does point to the name of Jesus as the jewel in the centre of this prayer.

HOLY MARY, MOTHER OF GOD

A certain young priest always brought his mother flowers on his own birthday. It was to say thanks for the gift of life! Jesus must have thanked his mother for the gift of human nature. 'When the fullness of time had come, God sent his Son, born of a woman' (Galatians 4:4). That text is short and straightforward, but startling in its implications.

Startling indeed, as I was to realise one day, when giving a lift to a Chinese man who had never heard of Christianity. I found myself trying to tell him about the Incarnation, and about Mary as Mother of God. In some strange way that I still do not understand, I found it difficult to state the plain fact that God became man and lived on this earth, and that we Christians have made him the centre of our religion. Telling it like that to a total newcomer made it all seem so unlikely and so impossible. I just could not blurt out: 'This is what I believe,' and took refuge in the impersonal statement: 'This is what Christians think.' Ever since, when I say 'Holy Mary, mother of God', I try to make it a genuine act of faith and acknowledge that for nine months the Virgin Mary carried the Son of God in her womb. This is the foundation of her greatness, and of all her other titles.

The poet Agnes Vollman speaks of Mary's longing to see the face of her yet unborn child.

> The Virgin longed to see the face
> of him she bore. She full of grace
> must wait nine months to gaze
> upon her God, her Christ, her Son.
> At last, O ever-mounting joy!
> He's born, her boy,

and lo, his sacred features
are like one other creature's.
His lips, his eyes, his brow,
formed in her till now,
are but her own,
hers alone.

...and our mother too

But Mary's motherhood stretches beyond Nazareth and reaches out to every believer in Christ. The Church is nothing more, and nothing less than Nazareth grown great. For on the day of Annunciation when Mary said yes to life for Jesus, she said yes to life for every one who would be one with him in his mystical body. We know a double motherhood in Mary. She gave birth to the historical physical being of Jesus. But then it was never the plan of God that Jesus would come alone. He was to bring with him all the members of his faith-body, the Church. 'Had it been otherwise,' says St Augustine, 'she would have conceived and brought forth a monster, a head without its members.'

Mary said yes to this whole Christ, and still goes on saying that yes. So when I bring her flowers in May, it is not only to honour her, but also to mark my own birthday in Christ. Under God, I am indebted to her for my very Christianity. There lies the reason for honouring her, a solid, substantial Christian one. This is why I've kept back the final verse of Agnes Vollman's poem, a verse which goes on to speak of that second longing in our Mother's heart, to see Christ once again in the face of every child of God.

The longing, is it stilled?
Ah no, for God hath willed
unto eternity

her task should be:
To mould his blessed features,
this time within all creatures.

Jesus Christ is the head of all humanity and the one who holds all things in being, and it is Mary who mothers and nurses that human creation in an unending cycle of love. St Augustine uses the daring expression that Mary is the 'mother and mould' of the Son of God and of the humanity graced by his divinity.

> Mary is the Mother of all the members of the Saviour, because by her charity she has co-operated in the birth of the faithful in the Church. Mary is the living mould of God, that is to say, it is in her alone that the God-man was naturally formed without losing a feature, so to speak, of his Godhead; and it is in her alone, that man can be properly and in a life-like way formed into God, so far as human nature is capable of this by the grace of Jesus Christ.

Far from seeing Mary as a rival to Jesus and to our Christian faith-practice, these two must be held in one embrace. The recitation of the Hail Mary and the contemplation of the sacred mysteries of the divine humanity in the Rosary go hand in hand and complement each other. The fifteen mysteries are simply fifteen reasons for saying: 'Blessed are you among women and blessed is the fruit of your womb, Jesus'.

HOLY MARY, PRAY FOR US

I was surprised to learn from other Christians that while they have no difficulty with the first half of the Hail Mary, they cannot accept the idea of asking Mary to pray for us. A Presbyterian remarked: 'Of course we honour Mary, mother of the Word made flesh. It's just that we don't believe in reaching out to the dead. We honour Mary and the saints for what the Lord did through them while they were on earth, but they cannot help us, nor can we reach them, now that they have entered into their rest.'

Much of this Protestant view stems from the Old Testament, which had a pretty vague understanding of life after death. Even if it did exist, it didn't seem to be worth much, just some kind of sleep not to be disturbed by the living. Pagan abuses and witchcraft prompted a ban on communication with the dead.

With the Good News of Jesus, all this changed. The dead are no longer defunct! Those who die in Christ, are the most alive of all members of the communion of saints. The new Catechism of the Catholic Church expresses it thus: 'The union of the wayfarers with the brethren who sleep in Christ is in no way interrupted, but on the contrary, according to the constant faith of the Church, this union is reinforced by the exchange of spiritual goods' (955).

We are encouraged to make friends with our departed loved ones here and now, so that later they may 'receive us into eternal dwellings' (Luke 1:69). Those who have won the victory are far from sitting in stately isolation from us 'poor banished children of Eve'. According to the Scriptures, they have been given 'authority over the nations' (Revelation 2:26). and they lift up 'vessels of gold filled with aromatic spices, which are the prayers of God's people'.

Being more united to Christ, those who dwell in heaven fix the whole Church more firmly in holiness. They do not cease to intercede with the Father for us, as they proffer the merits which they acquire on earth through the one mediator between God and men, Christ Jesus.... By their fraternal concern, our weakness is greatly helped. Exactly as Christian communion among our fellow pilgrims brings us closer to Christ, so our communion with the saints joins us to Christ, from whom as from a fountain-head issues all grace, and the life of the People of God itself. (*Constitution on the Church*, 49:50)

In the strict sense, of course, all Christian prayer is directed to the Most Holy Trinity, and in Jesus we go directly to the Father through the power of the Holy Spirit. But there is nothing in Scripture to prevent us going to holy people, either on earth or in heaven, to seek their intercession, remembering that it is the Christ in us that reaches out to the Christ in them, for 'flesh is of no avail, but faith working through love' (Galatians 5:6).

From the very earliest days, even as the first disciples waited behind locked doors for the outpouring of the Holy Spirit, we find that they are gathered with Mary. By her personal insights and profound prayer she would have helped to prepare them for this special occasion. To show how this intercession of Mary is still a living and active factor in the Church, Vatican II states:

This motherhood in the order of grace continues uninterruptedly from the consent which she loyally gave at the Annunciation and which she sustained without wavering beneath the cross, until the eternal fulfilment of all the elect. Taken up to heaven she did not lay aside this saving office, but by her manifold intercession continues to bring us the gifts of eternal salvation. Therefore the blessed Virgin is invoked in the Church under the titles of Advocate, Helper, Benefactress and Mediatrix. (*Constitution on the Church,* 62)

One of the most striking examples of the intercessory power of Mary is graphically illustrated on the face of the Miraculous Medal. Our Lady's hands are extended to the world with rays of light issuing from the jewels on her fingers. There are some jewels, however, which emit no light and Our Lady explained to St Catherine Labouré that these were the graces that people failed to ask for. On another occasion Mary appeared carrying a globe in her hands. 'This', she explained, 'symbolised the world itself, which God allowed her to carry and present before him. She covered it with her treasures and, like a tender and compassionate mother, kept it close to her heart, warming it with her love.'

Thinking about this little globe, Dom Helder Camara prayed thus:

> Mother, I rejoice at seeing this little globe in your hands! The globe is certainly small and I firmly believe that in it, our great problems, our agonies will be greatly diminished… I look again and I discover that this little globe has the power to diminish the afflictions which appear to us so immense and yet can be held in the palm of your hands.

Why, then, should anyone hesitate to ask this woman clothed with the sun, with the moon beneath her feet and a crown of twelve stars on her head, to pray for us?

> O Mary conceived without sin
> pray for us who have recourse to thee.

Us Sinners

St Dominic, the saint of the Rosary, made the daring cry that he would wish to be a stone in the mouth of hell in order to save sinners. In some of her apparitions Our Lady speaks of sinners and is seen to shed tears on their behalf. Jesus says that he came to save sinners and tells of the joy in heaven over one sinner that repents.

At Nevers in France, I was brought to the infirmary and shown the chair to which the sisters carried the dying Bernadette. As she lay there, gasping for breath, the last words she uttered were: 'Pray for me, a poor, poor sinner.' After the ecstasy of the apparitions and the miracles of soul and body which followed, Bernadette, herself the greatest 'miracle' of Lourdes, knew only how to hold out empty hands and beg for divine mercy.

At Fatima, Our Lady's own prayer was again for sinners: 'O my Jesus, forgive us our sins, save us from the fires of hell, and lead all souls to heaven, especially those who most need your mercy.'

> Sin is present in human history. Any attempt to ignore it or to give this dark reality other names would be futile. To try to understand what sin is, one must first recognise the profound relation of man to God, for only in this relationship is the evil of sin unmasked in its true identity as humanity's rejection of God and opposition to him, even as it continues to weigh heavy on human life and history. (*Catechism of the Catholic Church*, 386)

Scripture makes it clear that the battle between light and darkness is not a mere struggle against flesh and blood, but that behind it lurks the Evil One whom Jesus calls 'a murderer from the beginning'. There are those who would say that all this talk about the Devil is foolish. Yet take it out of the Gospels and a complete distortion of Christ's message and mission occurs. Padre Pio spent whole nights struggling with Satan. He would pray the Rosary all the time, saying it was the greatest weapon in this struggle. Frank Duff, founder of the Legion of Mary, would frequently say that those who deny the existence of the Devil are armchair Christians. They have no experience of the Evil One because they have never gone down to the battlefield. He told his followers that they were 'a Legion for service in the warfare which is perpetually waged by the Church against the world and its evil powers'.

> The power of Satan is nonetheless, not infinite. He is only a creature, powerful from the fact that he is pure spirit, but still a creature. He cannot prevent the building up of God's reign. Although Satan may act in the world out of hatred for God and his kingdom in Christ Jesus, and although his action may cause grave injuries, of a spiritual nature and, indirectly, even of a physical nature, to each man and to society, the action is permitted by divine providence which with strength and gentleness guides human and cosmic history. It is a great mystery that providence should permit diabolical activity, but 'we know that in everything, God works for good with those who love him' (Romans 8:28). (*Catechism of the Catholic Church*, 395)

NOW AND AT THE HOUR OF OUR DEATH

All life, like the Hail Mary itself, swings between two poles: now and the hour of death. One day they will meet as every Rosary brings them closer. Jesus came to take away the fear and the burden of death, to make it the gateway to eternal life. As we move on our pilgrim way round the beads, savouring the mysteries of the divine humanity, our own life, death and resurrection is given the grace of new direction and meaning.

For years, I was frightened of death; then I heard a wonderful, positive talk by Fr Peter Kirke, one of my own Dominican colleagues. Although an unwell man himself, he seemed, even in this valley of tears, to have his eyes on the unseen hills of heaven. He beckoned us towards those hills as he said so calmly: 'Don't let death cheat you. It is not something to submit to, in defeat, so much as something we hasten to with joy. Yield to the glory, and let death be the final offering of your life to God.'

It is finished!
This is what death was for Jesus, something he looked forward to with eagerness. The end was the finishing line: 'Father, I have finished the work you gave me to do.' When the end came, we are told that with a loud cry, 'It is finished', he gave up his spirit. That loud cry is a cry of the Holy Spirit, a shout of victory rather than a sigh of sorrow. The expression 'It is finished' could be misleading, as it could convey a sense of failure. The truth is that this was the battle cry of the Roman general when he sensed that the enemy had taken flight and that victory had been achieved. He would give a loud shout and have the trumpets sounded to let his soldiers know that the battle was won and the troops could return home with

pride and dignity. The better translation would be: 'It is accomplished!' or as an older version had it: 'It is consummated!'

I have continued to ponder Fr Peter's advice to the extent that, apart from the fear of how I might cope with a painful illness, death itself has lost all fear for me. I'd just be delighted at the thought of packing my bags and getting ready for heaven. I like the last words of Edel Quinn: 'Is Jesus coming?'

As we meditate in the Rosary on the passion and death of Jesus, we should all be growing into this awareness that death is the final battle with Satan and with darkness. It is our most splendid opportunity to make an oblation of our lives. Just as the priest at Mass lifts up the bread and the wine on the altar and prays that they may be consecrated, so should we lift up our own flesh and blood each day, saying: 'Here I am, Lord. I come to do your will. Take me, all that I am and all that I have, and make me into a living sacrifice acceptable in your sight. This, Lord, is my body given up to you'. If we live like that in the present, how glorious and victorious will be that moment when death is now!

In this sense, death can be a celebration – a going home. Friends may gather, but while they weep a little, there need be no regrets. They may have to let me slip away in peace and and know that there are angels present to lead me on this victory celebration.

Even if death finds me physically on my own I trust that I can be in spiritual contact with those I have loved in the vigour of young life. If at all possible I want to feel the touch of their hands, to see the love in their eyes, and to hear the sweet sound of their voices. But if that be not possible, I want right now, while still in my senses, to make a spiritual communion with them, a sacred covenant that they will stand by me in the supreme moment of death, as I would devoutly wish to be with any one of them if they should go before me. We have stood together as sinners praying to our Mother in life. How sweet it must be to hear those same voices around us in death.

Death is important and precious. I look forward to it as a young man looks forward to his bride as he watches her walk up the aisle to meet him on their wedding day. I don't want to let death overtake me by stealth and knock me over and wipe me out. I do not accept death as defeat, but as the final victory of life's battle. Like St Paul, I see it as the triumphal march to the place I have longed for all my little life.

Bells may ring from the chapel tower, but I want them to be wedding bells. The music I would like is that symphony which sounds like canons booming and fireworks piercing the night sky. I want to go out in a blaze of glory. Even if my frail flesh is worn and my physical strength exhausted, as was Christ's on the Cross, I want to go like him, crying: 'It is accomplished!'

When I say 'Hail Mary'

When I say 'Holy Mary, mother of God, pray for us sinners now and at the hour of our death', I remind myself of how eagerly Jesus looked forward to the accomplishment of the Father's will and the salvation of sinners by the sacrifice of his own life on Calvary. Behind the seeming aloneness and desolation of death, there is the hidden splendour of the soul that lives in a spirit always ready to yield to glory. Motorists are familiar with those road signs which read: 'Yield to oncoming traffic'. I hope that my old body-carriage may always be ready to give way with delight to the oncoming traffic of the angels.

Don't cry too much!

So please don't cry too much when I wave goodbye. Don't sing a dirge-like 'Alone with none but thee, my God, I journey on my way'. I want to go marching out to glory, and want to have a part with Jesus in the work of preparing a place for you. So blow the trumpets; let off the fireworks; let the wedding march begin. Death is swallowed up in victory. I want my death to be a living sacrifice, a glorious surrender into the hands of a living, loving God. Amen! Amen! Amen!

I can still hear my own Father's loud cry when, every night after the Rosary, he would pray:

Jesus, Mary and Joseph, I give you my heart and my soul.
Jesus, Mary and Joseph, assist me now and in my last agony.
Jesus, Mary and Joseph, may I breathe forth my soul in
peace with you. Amen.

He taught us at a tender age to make an offering of our lives, and how to breathe forth our souls in peace. In their own way our parents taught us to pray like St Francis of Assisi: 'Welcome, Sister Death.'

Strange how the simple 'Holy Mary, Mother of God, pray for us' brings together the now of this moment and the now of death. The secret of a happy last hour would seem to be to go on living joyously in the sacrament of the present moment, not worrying about the past and likewise not looking anxiously ahead. Helen Mallicaot has words that can help:

I Am
I was regretting the past
and fearing the future.
Suddenly my Lord was speaking:
'My name is – I am.'
He paused. I waited. He continued:
When you live in the past
with its mistakes and regrets,

It is hard. I am not there.
My name is not – I was.
When you live in the future,
with its problems and fears,
It is hard. I am not there.
My name is not – I will be.
When you live in this moment,
it is not hard.
I am here. My name is – I am.

Lord, give me the grace to live in this present moment, to savour the word you wish to say to me in this situation here and now. Help me not to be concerned about the past or want to 'see the distant scene', but know how to take the next simple step with grace, and to abandon myself to your loving providence.

My past, O Lord, to thy mercy.
My present, O Lord, to thy love.
My future, O Lord, to thy providence.

'Holy Mary, pray for us sinners now, and at the hour of our death. Amen.'

THE SECRETS OF THE ROSARY

If you find the word 'mystery' off-putting, then settle for the fifteen secrets of the Rosary, for the word 'mystery' means secret in the original Greek. Like all secrets, the Rosary secrets are precious and powerful, and they bind together those who treasure them, making them precious to each other as well. We share these mysteries with Jesus, and with Mary, who 'pondered them in her heart'. As we rest in them, we are being brought into communion with those sacred persons who first lived and treasured them.

The mysteries or secrets of the Rosary are those sacred events in the life story of Jesus which were lived out in Palestine two thousand years ago, but are as priceless and as precious today as they were then. Because Jesus is the Son of God, there is an infinite dimension to everything about him. He just can't be yesterday's man. As scripture says, he is 'yesterday, today, the same forever.' Everything about him has a deathless, timeless, limitless quality which means that the events of his life are never out-of-date or out of place. They are not just past history, but ever-present, and they belong to all. Therein lies their secret, their mystery.

Human history – divine mystery
History speaks to the fleeting emotion, to the wandering imagination, to the memory and to the reasoning mind. Mystery touches the depths of soul and spirit and draws us into secrets locked in the mind of God himself. 'We keep the past for pride,' said the Irish patriot, Tom Kettle. Legitimate human pride, no doubt. Divine mystery, however, is an ever-present, personal, practical reality revealed only to those who, like Jesus, are meek and humble of heart.

Detail of a painting by Pisanello of a pilgrim on his way to Compostella, complete with cockle-shell, staff and beads. This shows the Rosary at an early stage of development, clearly a distinctive aid to the contemplative spirit of the pilgrim.

This beautiful painting, attributed to Gossaert, highlights the Beads and the Book of the Scriptures, the two elements that go to make up the fullness of the Rosary.

As Our Lord went through the various stages of his life, he built up a powerhouse of divine life and power which is stored up as a source of energy for the whole people of God. We think of a nuclear generator or an electricity grid which stores up power, heat and light for a complete range of activities at remote points of application. Just so, Christian power, with its divine life and love, comes to humanity through grace of Jesus, head of the whole human network. He lived these mysteries for our sake and they are alive and active, influencing the lives of those who now touch the Saviour in faith, hope and love.

The realisation of this fact is of immense value to those who try to interact with the mysteries of Jesus in the Rosary. If they are mere stories from the past, and if Christ is a figure who has simply walked through this world and is now dead and gone, then the events of his life have little significance for us. There is nothing in them to command our attention, nothing, to light the way and no power for spiritual lift-off. The new Catechism of the Catholic Church, with an eye on the Letter to the Hebrews, treats of this under the heading 'Our communion in the mysteries of Jesus'...: 'All Christ's riches "are for every individual and are everybody's property"' (John Paul II, *Redemptor hominis*). Christ did not live his life for himself, but *for us*. He remains ever... 'in the presence of God on our behalf, bringing before him all that he lived and suffered for us'. (Heb 9:24) (519)

In him we live and move and have our being

I've always been fascinated by St Paul's claim to be living out the mystery of Jesus in his own flesh and blood, daring to say that he completes and makes up in his own body all that is wanting in the mystery of Christ. How, we might ask, can anything be lacking in the complete and finished work of Jesus? Does the Lord somehow draw us into his own redeeming work? The French writer Leon Bloy, noting this stunning paradox, remarked that 'we have the privilege of being needed by him who has need of no one.'

It is not only Paul, and people like St Francis and Padre Pio, who have borne the wounds of Christ. In a sense, all of us bear these wounds. We live out in our flesh the life, death and glory of Christ. 'In him, we live and move and have our being.' In the Rosary, we are called to ponder the mysteries, not only in our minds, but to the extent of participation, so that by delving into them and imitating what they contain, we may obtain what they promise. Rosary meditation is never a clinical consideration of some abstract truth. Neither is it a journey which terminates in the darkness and the void. Jesus came that we might have life and have it to the full.

The Catechism continues: 'Christ enables us *to live in him,* all that he lived in himself, and *he lives it in us.* "By his Incarnation, he, the Son of God, has in a certain way united himself with each man" (*Gaudium et spes,* 22)' (521).

Anyone wishing to pursue this matter, so vital to the secrets of the Rosary, would do well to study the teaching of St John Eudes, a summary of which can be found in the Office of Readings for Friday of Week Thirty-three. Following St Paul, he writes:

> We ought to imitate and complete in ourselves the various states and mysteries of Christ. We should frequently beseech him to bring them to perfection in us and in the whole Church. For though in his person, they are perfected, the mysteries of Jesus have not yet reached completion in us, his members, nor in the Church, which is his mystical body. The Son of God plans to make us sharers in his mysteries and, in a certain manner, continues them in us and in the Church by the

graces, which he has decided to communicate to us, and the effects which he wishes to bring about in us through these mysteries. This is how he wishes to complete his mysteries in us. They will not reach their completion until the end of the time which he has decreed, that is, until the end of the world.

Those who wish to advance in the secret ways of the Rosary will bear in mind that there is something more important than the recitation of prayers and the effort to meditate. There is the divine action of the Spirit, weaving the golden thread of Christ's life into the fabric of our lives. There will indeed be times when recitation and meditation weary us. Then is the time to surrender to the process of letting the Lord himself touch our lives.

With the spread in adoration of the Blessed Sacrament exposed, the Rosary is often prayed aloud before the sacred presence. It is helpful in these circumstances to focus on the person of Jesus himself, realising that he is the first secret, the prime mystery revealed to us. All the mysteries of his life are focused on and crystallised in the Eucharist which might be compared to the sun, around which the other heavenly bodies of our universe revolve. My own practice is to invite people to sit up and rest his presence. I ask them to look in love and to listen in humility. For this purpose, the text I use before taking up the meditation on the individual mysteries of the Rosary is Matthew 11:25, 30:

> Jesus exclaimed, 'I bless you Father, Lord of heaven and earth, for hiding these things from the learned and the clever and revealing them to mere children... Come to me all you who labour and are overburdened, and I will give you rest. Shoulder my yoke and learn from me, for I am gentle and humble in heart, and you will find rest for your souls.'

THE LITTLE SHARED PRAYER GROUP

The Gaelic name for the Rosary is An Paidrín Páirteach, which might be translated the Little Shared Prayer, or, more accurately, the Little Partnered Prayer. It is so called because it is a sharing with Mary in those 'things which she treasured in her heart', but it is also a prayer we make in partnership with others. The Rosary can profitably be said in the solitude of our room or travelling the roads. But there is a special grace that goes with joining with others for its recitation.

This may take the form of meeting up with a close friend, a prayer partner, gathering as a family or, as is increasingly the case these days, associating on a regular basis with a small, closely-knit prayer group.

Many of these groups meet in the home, with friends and neighbours. This kind of open house is becoming a modern type of family Rosary. With the imperious demands of television, it is not easy to assemble any one family on a nightly basis. These extended neighbourhood societies are growing rapidly, taking on a slightly more formal character than the traditional family Rosary. The Bible is given a place of honour, and passages suited to the occasion are used.

Leaders emerge naturally and a kind of bush-phone system holds the individuals together and helps them link up with other groups in a kind of spirit-filled network. Meditations for each mystery and hymns are usually used between the decades and someone is appointed to give a short talk. Unlike the usual church Rosary where a priest would lead and leave, at these groups meetings tend to spill over into ministries of counselling and healing among the members themselves. Most groups end with a simple social, tea and biscuits or whatever may be the custom of the place.

Certain guidelines for the development of such groups were noted by Pope Paul VI in *Marialis cultus*. He mentions certain elements which would be helpful in the more fruitful praying of the Rosary in these situations. As they start in the English language with the letter S, they are easily recalled:

Scripture,
Silence, between decades,
Song and music,
Sharing of experiences
Spontaneous prayer.

Experience has proved the fruitfulness of these suggestions. But there is no need to be worried if they do not all materialise. The Holy Spirit breathes where and when it wills.

Group or shared prayer of this kind brings to bear on the Rosary certain qualities which greatly enrich it. The members learn to live together with one heart and one mind. Over and above this simple human dimension is the added factor of the grace of Christ by which the members grow into a supernatural, life-giving structure which builds up the whole People of God.

The Rosary Confraternity

It would of course be desirable that these informal groups be affiliated to the worldwide Rosary Confraternity, which is the official society of the Rosary, endowed by the Church with many privileges and indulgences.

It was in the year 1486 that Michael de Insulis (François de Lille OP) appeared in the University of Cologne at the time of public debates, with his Defence of the Rosary Confraternity. He made it clear that fraternity or fellowship in the Holy Spirit was an essential element of Christian prayer. His scriptural inspiration was verse 3 of Psalm 118; 'I share as companion with all those who keep your law.'

This sharing is not confined to the saying of prayers, but embraces concern for the material and bodily welfare of one's companions. It is primarily concerned with the sharing of the supernatural values, which arises from intercessory prayer and ministry. The members are asked to make a complete consecration of themselves to the Blessed Virgin, allowing her, in her gracious wisdom, to share out the combined treasury of grace with the whole group. We can see from this, that what we are talking about in the true Rosary fellowship, is not a question of counting heads, or being together in one place or united in one voice. The oneness aimed at is a oneness in Christ.

After pondering this original thrust of the Rosary Confraternity, I composed a blessing for the beads, which begins:

> God, our Father, may the circle of these beads be a sign of our coming together in the Body of Christ. May the circle be a reminder of Jesus in the midst of us, presenting his wounds on our behalf before your face.

The great preacher of the Rosary Confraternity, William Pepin, a contemporary of Michael de Insulis, has left us a splendid collection of sermons on this subject of the shared spirituality of the Rosary. He pointed to the text of Luke 15:31: 'All that I have, is yours...' which comes from the story of the Prodigal Son. The father gives the elder son a powerful lesson in the matter of sharing with his brother. In those words, 'All that is mine, is yours', the father is telling him to assume the authority of an elder brother.

The generous father tells his first-born that he is perfectly entitled, indeed obliged, to go into the family treasure room, and to take out what is necessary for the younger needy one. He is being challenged to put the cloak of mercy on his brother's back, to put the shoes on his feet, and the ring of loving relationship on his finger. The cloak is for protection, the shoes are for freedom – only slaves went barefoot. The ring symbolises love, friendship, covenant relationship. These three are the qualities of confraternity, united brother/sisterhood, which brings with it genuine respect and generous sharing.

Far from the begrudgery of one who has 'slaved all these years', the long-standing elders should realise that everything the father has is already their own, and that they are perfectly entitled to kill the fatted calf themselves and to celebrate their brothers and sisters. They claim that authority, not for their own selfish interests, but for the common good of all.

This is the spirit that should animate any sound Christian prayer group and form the basis of genuine Christian leadership. The Book of Revelation speaks of those who win the victory and are given the right to share the throne. Christian leaders in prayer movements or in any form of ministry have no right to disclaim that God-given authority. If, out of false humility, they do so, then others suffer by their failure to act as true elder brothers or sisters.

'So', continues William Pepin, 'every member of the Rosary Confraternity should leave behind the self-pitying slave mentality, and step out with head held high, not only to claim personal inheritance, but to share it in a spirit of Christian fellowship. As princes and princesses of the royal blood we enjoy innumerable privileges which, however, bring with them obligations of love and service in the royal household of the Confraternity.'

True devotion to Mary

Anyone familiar with this original teaching will see the source from which St Louis Marie de Montfort drew to form his own True Devotion to Mary. We know from the latter's own words, that what troubled him was that in his day there did not exist any true Rosary Confraternity. So he set himself about remedying the matter. Little wonder that the Provincial of the Dominican Order commended him, in this statement still in existence: 'We, the Provincial of the Order of Preachers, do certify, that Louis Grignion de Montfort, Brother of our Third Order, preaches everywhere and with much zeal, edification and fruit, the Confraternity of the Rosary in all the Missions which he gives continually in the towns and country places.'

Once, when discussing this matter with the founder of the Legion of Mary, Frank Duff told me that had he been aware of this background to the Rosary Confraternity, he would have made it the basis for the Legion spirituality. The idea of beginning with a serious consecration and entrustment to Mary, and the concept of spiritual sharing and participating, are essential elements common to the Legion and to the Rosary Confraternity.

Any Rosary group operating today, or, indeed, anyone who prays the Rosary, can only enhance their prayer by affiliation to the Confraternity. The apostolate of the Rosary is not limited to roping more people in, but must reach out with a whole programme of spiritual enrichment and evangelisation.

To be affiliated, a person's name must be enrolled on the register in a church where the Confraternity has been established. Members are also asked to act as elder sisters or brothers by sharing their spiritual treasure with the other members, and remembering their intentions. The result of this is that sharing members belong in the very best sense of the word, and never walk alone again. They share in all the prayers and good works of the members of the Confraternity world-wide.

Do not fear that in placing in Mary's hands the fruit of your works to be shared among others, you may lose out. You are dealing with a gracious Queen, who will treat you like the prince or princess you are. Blessed Alan de la Roche points out that since we are dealing with spiritual food, and not with material things, sharing with others does not mean loss. The more mouths there are for bodily bread the less there is to go round. The bread of heaven, on the other hand, kneaded with the yeast of faith, hope and love, increases the more it is divided.

Members are asked to say, at the very least, the complete round of fifteen decades within the week. To encourage a slower pace and a lingering rhythm, they are given the privilege of breaking up the decades any way they wish. They must also meditate or contemplate the mysteries to the best of their ability.

Over and above the plenary indulgence granted to all who pray the Rosary in the family or in a group or religious community, there are special plenary indulgences for members of the Rosary Confraternity on the day of admission, on the feasts of Christmas, Easter, the Annunciation, the Assumption, the Immaculate Conception, the Presentation of Our Lord in the Temple and the Rosary itself. Further information can be had from any Dominican priory or regional Rosary centre.

THE HEALING LIGHT OF THE ROSARY

There's healing in touching the very beads themselves, a lowly healing maybe, yet something basic and instinctive. When all around is collapsing and the centre cannot hold, it is something to latch on to. 'Worry beads' are universal. They let the sense of touch do its healing work. The fretful child lulls itself to sleep clutching a much-loved teddy bear. A frightened adult reaches for a comforting hand in times of stress. Heaven has its own psychology, and the Rosary beads must have a high rating in its pain department!

Robert Llewelyn, formerly chaplain to the Julian of Norwich Society, writes of the Rosary as an instrument of healing:

> Go round the whole body, making each part an object of attention or awareness, saying the Rosary prayers at the same time. Thus, be aware of the heart centre. Let your mind descend into the heart. You are directing the healing energy of love to that part of your body. Then go round your body, mentally taking one or two beads for each part, shoulder, arms, hands, the brow, the face, the jaw... In this way, you bring healing to every part of your body, and thus to every part of yourself, that body-soul complex which makes up each one of us. Perhaps, one half of the hospital beds in the country would be emptied, if everyone were to spend fifteen minutes on this each day...!

Not just something, but someone!
Something to hold on to, indeed. But more importantly, someone to hold on to! It is the Nurse of heaven who holds the

other end of the golden string. 'Nurse of the shining white Lamb' as an Irish poet called her, Mary invites us to grasp this lifeline. The beads enshrine her precious and sacred secrets, and they hold the healing blood medicine of the Saviour.

Down the centuries, the beads have been used in the ministry of healing. St Louis Bertrand, the Spanish apostle of New Granada, was accustomed to carrying a large Rosary round his neck, and one of his favourite practices was to place it about the neck of sick persons. The chronicler tells how, when he did this with the Countess of Albayda, her illness immediately vanished and her strength was restored. Many miraculous favours were granted to those who reverently used Rosaries blessed by this saint. After his return to Valencia, he gave a Rosary to a friend and told him to preserve it with reverence 'because in the Indies this Rosary cured the sick, converted sinners, and, I think, also raised the dead to life.'

On another occasion, he spoke more decidedly to a spiritual confidante, saying directly. 'God in His mercy granted that this Rosary should raise the dead to life.' Thus his devotion to the Rosary betrayed him into revealing a miracle he had sought to conceal, the raising of a girl to life during his South American mission. The report spread among the natives and reached Valencia, but the saint would neither acknowledge nor deny its truth. Once, when asked so directly that he could not hedge, he replied: 'What makes you ask such a question? God does what a blacksmith would do, when making an iron tool. He has made many suitable pieces of material and selects the one he pleases, although all are fit for his purpose.'

Healing blessing for the beads
Healing figures highly with many Rosary groups today, and it is usual to give a blessing for this purpose to the beads which

the members use freely in the manner of St Louis Bertrand. As part of this blessing the following words occur:

> Father of mercy, heal the sick who touch these beads with faith, hope and love, and may power go out from the Gospel mysteries, which we contemplate and celebrate to transform us into the likeness of Jesus, and make us strong with all the strength which comes from his divine humanity.

With the beads around the neck, or in the hands of the sick person, I like to read the text from Mark 5:

> There was a woman who suffered terribly even though she had been to many doctors... She touched his cloak and her bleeding stopped at once... Jesus knew that power had gone out from him, so he turned round in the crowd and asked: 'Who touched my clothes?'

Jesus, whom we touch in every mystery of the Rosary, is still the source of power, and the author of healing. As we make contact with the simple string of beads, it is as if we were touching the hem of his garment, the very edge of eternity.

I always like to place the focus of healing on touching the person of the Lord rather than the actual beads. I invite people to enter into the contemplative flow of the prayer and to make contact with the life-giving mysteries which are the soul of the Rosary. I composed the following prayer which brings our personal experience into line with the life-experience of the Lord himself:

> Jesus, Son of the living God, I desire to recall the memory of your healing life, death and glory. Through

the power of your saving mysteries, touch every area of my being. Let my coming into this world be renewed by your own birth at Bethlehem. Let your precious death remove from me all fear of death. Grant me to know the power which comes from your glorious resurrection and ascension into heaven.

Through the grace of these Rosary mysteries, touch every area of my life and be Lord of all that I am and all that I have.

O Mary, who first opened yourself to this new creation, pray for me, a sinner, that I may be renewed in the love of my Lord.

Père Bernard of Toulouse, in his classic *Le Triple Rosaire,* tells members of the Confraternity to take the oil from the lamp burning before the Rosary altar and bring it to the sick. He cites the example of the members in Milan who anoint themselves with this oil and receive a great number of cures. He tells them to invoke the names of Jesus and Mary as they do so. He also gave a form of blessing to go with the anointing:

May the Lord Jesus Christ heal you from this illness and anxiety, through the intercession of the Blessed Virgin Mary, in the Name of the Father, the Son and the Holy Spirit. Amen.

A colleague of mine relates how the old women of Tralee, in the south-west of Ireland, would pull down the lamp at the Rosary altar and dip cotton wool in it to take home. They must have been acting under some old instruction, though no one was quite sure and nobody dared stop them or ask why.

When time is available, it is not wise to rush into a situation, applying the oil or the beads right away. There is the danger of attachment to the material objects in themselves, though indeed the Church has a long-standing tradition of imparting blessings to them. I like to first rest with the patients, endeavouring to listen with the ears of Jesus, looking with his eyes and reaching out with something of his touch.

That demands faith in my own Christian charism and helps to evoke the same attitude in the person before me. Having listened and looked awhile I bless the beads of the sick and invite them to join me in saying at least one decade of the Rosary. I tell those concerned, patient and friends, to pray very slowly and peacefully, resting in the names of Jesus and Mary. I ask for a pause at the Holy Name, saying: 'When you say *Jesus,* breathe out all your fear and trouble. While you breathe in, let the healing love of the Lord fill your whole being, body, mind and spirit.'

I tell people also that this invocation of the name of Jesus is in itself a spiritual communion, a kind of little liturgy. 'As at Mass, bring all your cares and troubles and unite them with the offering of Jesus on the altar. Then press your wounds to the precious and glorious wounds of Christ in a spiritual communion.'

This is embodied in the prayer said after each decade:

God, our Father, we press our open wounds to the precious wounds of Jesus your Son, that your will and ours be one. Through these shared wounds, may we be healed and bring your healing love to others, that all may be enriched in the fullness of love, through Jesus, the Divine Humanity. (See my booklet, *The Healing Light of the Rosary,* available from the Rosary Apostolate, Tallaght, Dublin 24.)

I will heal you through each other

The Rosary meditations from the above-mentioned booklet have this refrain running through it: 'I will heal you through each other.' This promise of the Lord touches upon the fact that healing is not confined to extraordinary charismatic leaders, but that a normative low-key healing is always at work in the body of Christ. This operates as an interactive process among the members of a praying group. That is why a loving community spirit is encouraged. Expectant faith and unwavering hope in those present can make wonderful things happen. Because of its normality this ordinary healing process may well be the most precious gift of all. While we thank God for the highly graced ones in the healing ministry we must not, in our rush to meet the stars, miss the flowers beneath our feet.

Apart from actual prayer sessions, which usually meet once a week, members keep in touch with each other, so that healing is an ongoing thing. Listening to a friend in trouble, being available at the other end of a phone, cooking meals, caring for sick children or aged parents, co-operating graciously with those in the office or workshop – these are essential elements in the whole healing structure.

When we think of the hurt done by harsh words, anger, pride, arrogance and lack of forgiveness, then it becomes obvious that their opposites, love, kindness and consideration, are basic to the ministry of healing. How many ulcers, headaches, heartaches and sheer mental torture and sexual pain could be avoided if people would just be loving towards each other. Jesus is still the Divine Physician, and Mary is the kindly Nurse of the sick. With their honoured presence in home, workshop, or community, healing is never distant.

So I don't wait for some great character to come to town . Healing begins with me! It is in my heart and in my hands! 'I will heal you through each other.'

The Rosary has its vocal prayers, though indeed they are never merely vocal. Behind the words there is the rhythm, the romance and the reason already mentioned. But that's very much the ABC, the beginners' class in the school of the Rosary. We have to advance to the class of meditation and move on to final stages of rest, relaxation and recreation. That's a few more R's added to our rhythm, romance and reason!

Meditation is the 'in-thing'. Many people are seeking a guru to teach them. They are prepared to travel to the East in search of a mantra, or pay out big money for a weekend at some posh hotel to learn the secret of meditation. Fine, but the Rosary has it already and in a blissfully simple Christian form. Moreover, it is not all about emptying oneself into the ocean of the void. It may start there, but it goes on to an infilling. If we come with empty vessels, it is only to be filled with the love of Christ and with the outpouring of his Holy Spirit.

Rosary meditation provides an effective way of combining all that is best in human culture and the counsel of the Lord Jesus. The very act of holding the beads and repeating the rhythmic sounds of the Paters and Aves, starts the stilling process of the soul, and helps us take on the mind of Christ. Centreing ourselves with a loving regard on the persons of Jesus and Mary brings with it a love-dimension which settles the troubled heart. Meditating on the mysteries of the Rosary is not a question of painful pulling of the mind into line, but rather a kind of thinking in the heart. Like the beloved disciple resting on the Lord's breast at the Supper table, we have ceased from labour, and are re-collecting our spent forces.

In this twin study of Saints Jerome and Alesius, by Mantegna, both are portrayed contemplating the Crucifix with the aid of the beads. Attaching the Crucifix to the beads is a later stage. Note the carrying case for ink hanging from Jerome's belt.

Thirteenth-century picture showing the use of Beads. The Sienese character carrying beads and cooking pot belonged to a society caring for poor sick.

> The world is too much with us,
> Late and soon;
> Getting and spending,
> We lay waste our powers

Rosary meditation takes us out of the rat race of getting and spending and helps concentrate our powers on the Lord. Busy executives learn to sit quietly on the commuter train with their beads in their hands and their minds on the divine mysteries. Fr Cussen, the Dominican who preached the Rosary all over Australia, tells of one fretful commuter looking over his paper at a fellow passenger across from him, who appeared to be snoozing in the corner. 'O'Hara's a tiger for sleep!' he'd say, only to be told one day, 'O'Hara's not asleep, he's away with Jesus in Galilee!'

Time magazine showed pictures of the lovely meditation gardens which have been incorporated into many large industrial and commercial firms in Japan. Managers come to work early in the morning to sit and meditate in these havens of peace. They find that this steadies their nerves and helps them deal with problems and projects throughout the day.

An oriental passenger next to me on a plane was fingering a string of small, beautifully coloured stones as we took off. 'We use them', he said, 'to make us calm and settle us down to sleep.' I showed him the large Rosary beads which I had in my own hands, and we rejoiced at how East and West were joined with a string of beads.

The first requirement for meditation is stillness, stillness of the body but, more importantly, stillness of the heart. 'Be still and know that I am God.' 'Be still before the Lord and wait for him' (Psalm 37:7). The New American Bible puts it forcibly: 'Leave it to the Lord.' It is a kind of letting go and letting God. Psalm 131 invites us to rest like a child in the arms of the Lord: 'I have stilled and quieted my soul, like a child quieted at its mother's breast.'

Christian contemplation does not end in the mind or the heart. It is not merely a mental exercise, but goes on to engage the whole personality and to overflow in love of others. The fruit of Rosary meditation shows in the transformation it effects. The words of St Paul in Romans 12:2 are pertinent: 'Do not be conformed to the world, but be transformed by the renewal of your mind, that you may prove what is the will of God, what is good and acceptable and perfect.'

As we look to the Lord, we radiate something of his glory. It is told of Moses that on coming down from the mountain where he had conversed with God, the people could see the radiance on his face, so much so that he had to keep a veil over it. This is what St Paul was referring to when he wrote: 'All we, with unveiled faces, reflecting the glory of the Lord, are being changed into his likeness from one degree of glory to another; for this comes from the Lord who is the Spirit' (2 Corinthians 3:18).

As we look at Jesus in each mystery of the Rosary, we too are being changed into his likeness. Meditation or contemplation, which is the simplest form of this exercise, is nothing more than this looking, this lingering in love with the Lord. All one has to do is recall the scene, picture Jesus in the inner heart and recognise his presence, enfolding you in his love. Underpinning all fifteen secrets of the Rosary is this one all-pervading secret, that as you surrender to its graced process you are being renewed, restored, revitalised, transformed. Do not be diverted from this lingering in love with the Lord himself by the multiplicity of mysteries and vocal prayers. A lot of things in this book and in sermons on prayer, are simply the gathering of bricks and boards for the building of your house. When the labour of building is over, just sit at the fire and enjoy your home and dream along with the lover of your soul.

This kind of prayer has been described by Caroline Carney in one of her poems:

> Prayer is the tide which returns,
> running full and free with God,
> to flow out into our days,
> taking us through the rich park lands of Summer,
> or the desolate forlorn terrain of Winter
> or the pleasant diversities of Spring and Autumn.
> Prayer is the dream,
> we dream along with God,
> as locked in the eternal rhythm,
> we move sweetly into love,
> the love for which all has well been lost
> and won, as we enter Paradise at last.

When the time for contemplative rest comes, there need not be any straining after thoughts or mental images. Let the Spirit waft you along. Dream along with God, and you will wake up transformed. You will come out of the darkness, reflecting his glory.

The simple sound

What the monk Cassian calls 'the poverty of the single word.' can help to unlock the many secrets of the Rosary. The names Mary or Jesus, or Abba Father, may gather all your thoughts and desires into one simple sound. Or you may find peace in the rhythmic wave-like balance of the Ave: 'Blessed art thou… Blessed is the fruit of thy womb…'. As you yield yourself to the mystery, breathe in the healing grace that is stored up in it like a balm for soul and body. The very simplicity and apparent monotony of the oft-repeated words, far from being boring, becomes the key to meditation and contemplation.

The very familiarity of the well-worn paths of the Rose Garden sets the spirit free to wander and to wonder.

In this chapter I have interchanged the terms meditation and contemplation as is the modern popular practice. In classical Christian teaching, however, the two processes are distinct. 'Meditation engages thought, imagination, emotion and desire. This mobilisation of faculties is necessary in order to deepen our convictions of faith, prompt the conversion of our heart and strengthen our will to follow Christ' (*Catechism of the Catholic Church*, 2708).

Many will pray the Rosary in this way, conjuring up images of Jesus as an infant, in his terrible agony and crucifixion, or in the glory of his resurrection. They will labour at drawing out the virtues that flow from these mysteries, making sure to imitate what they contain and obtain what they promise.

Intimacy and rest

Contemplation, however, is a more restful experience during which the soul finds itself incapable of mental labour and desires only to look and to listen, to sit and to sigh in silence. Certainly there will be no rush to get through, no 'lust for finishing' and no panic about distractions. A certain preacher was often heard to remark that the Rosary is one of the prayers you can say with distractions! Perhaps he meant that in the contemplative mode the spirit can be left free to wonder and to wander, to 'dream along with God'. St Teresa says: 'Contemplative prayer in my opinion is nothing else than a close sharing between friends. It means taking time frequently to be alone with him who knows and loves us.'

People sometimes worry that they can no longer keep their minds on any distinct mystery. They forget what mystery they are at. Before they know where they are, the Rosary is over.

This is not necessarily something to worry about. It may well be that such souls have passed beyond the labour of meditation. They have moved on to the stage of contemplation where attention is no longer on words or thoughts, but on the person of the Lord himself – letting him love them just as they are.

Fr Bernard, the sixteenth-century Dominican of Toulouse, writes of how the Rosary becomes simpler and more profound as one makes acts of love, adoration, and praise. The soul moves into intimacy and union, looking to God more as lover than as Lord. 'Those', he says, 'who pray the Rosary with a high degree of contemplation should not be constrained to make complicated meditations, for that would be to pay their spiritual debts in silver, when they should be trading in gold. They are no longer helped by that searching which is peculiar to meditation, but must use the talent God has given in restful prayer, like the infant asleep on its mother's breast, or like the lover locked in her lover's arms.' This recalls the words of Hosea: 'It is the Lord who speaks: I am going to lure her and lead her out into the wilderness and speak to her heart' (2:14).

It can be seen how very natural this growth in divine intimacy is, by observing how love develops in ordinary daily living. When a young couple become engaged, they spend lots of time talking, discussing and making plans for their future. They meditate in their minds and labour in the sweat of their brow. As children arrive, they struggle to spend time with each other. Action takes over from rest. But then, in the evening of life, they find time again to be alone. They do not return to the busied conversation of youth. They want to be silent and still. One often hears after the death of a spouse: 'I miss him. Half of me is gone. I feel a terrible emptiness without him. Not that he ever said much, but I always knew he was there.

He would sit in his corner and I would be across the fire from him. We would just look at each other.'

That's how it is with those who have grown into the contemplative way of the Rosary. They have gone beyond words and meditation. Their attention is to the person of Jesus rather than to any graphic detail or particular mystery. They have discovered the true secret of the Rosary, 'how to linger in love with the Lord'.

Mary Comes to Teach Us

The Lady smiles

At Lourdes, Our Lady appeared high up in the cliff-face and smiled down graciously on the little Bernadette. 'The Lady looked at me. She smiled on me and said: "Come closer".' Something like this happens with each of us as we meet Our Lady in prayer. She looks at us. We look at her. When people asked Bernadette if the lady in the grotto looked at anyone else but herself, she answered firmly: 'Yes, indeed she does. She looks all around the crowd and stops at some, as if they are old familiar friends.' And that's just what we are in the Rosary, Mary's old and not so old familiar friends! When we take up the beads, heaven and earth are joined and the Queen of heaven looks down, smiles and calls us closer. Personally, there are times when all formal prayer and preaching become too much. I lie still then, and let the sweet mother nurse me. And when I think that death might soon steal upon me, I pray softly: 'Mother, look upon me. Smile on me now, and at the hour of death, call me home to be always near you.' When that time comes I may not be able to finger the beads. They'll be what they were for the dying man in the London air raid – something, someone to hold on to.

The sacredness of the Rosary comes home when we realise that, at Lourdes, Our Lady actually took the lead in saying it with Bernadette. Here are Bernadette's own words: 'On each foot she wore a yellow rose; her Rosary was the same colour... I wanted to make the sign of the cross but I could not lift my hand to my forehead; it fell back. Then the Lady crossed herself. I again tried, and although my hand was trembling, I was eventually able to make the sign of the cross. I began to say my Rosary. The Lady slipped the beads through her fingers, but she did not move her lips…'.

She looked at me

Bernadette was a very poor, illiterate, asthmatic, pragmatic, peasant child, who knew absolutely nothing about scripture. When her sister found her in a trance-like state beside the River Gave at the dumping-ground in Massabielle, she thought that Bernadette was dying, and got friends to help carry her home.

'What happened?' asked her worried mother.

'I saw something white in Massabielle,' replied Bernadette.

'What do you mean, something white?'

'It was a white thing', replied the child.

'Like a white sheet, a white cloud, what do you mean, white?'

'No', said the child, after very careful consideration. 'It was just a white thing'. And after more thought, 'it was shaped like a woman.'

'Did it say anything to you, then?'

'No.'

'Did it do anything?' asked her bewildered mother.

'No', said Bernadette, 'it just – it just looked at me the way one person looks at another.'

At the time, Bernadette did not know the names of the mysteries or, indeed, that there were any such things as mysteries. She simply looked and observed that the lady looked at her. That profound look, that steadfast gaze was enough for herself and for those who stood by and watched. 'We could see nothing' they stated, 'but that look on the face of Bernadette was enough to convince us that she was in touch with a world beyond.' One of the most profound reasons for saying the Rosary is just that. It keeps us in touch with the world beyond.

The open heart at Fatima

As at Lourdes, Mary defined herself: *'I am the Immaculate Conception';* at Fatima, she named herself again: *'I am the Lady of the Rosary'.* What high status for this humble prayer!

Fatima brings us a step further into the secrets of the Rosary. On one occasion, Mary opened her hands and revealed her heart. With one hand she pointed to the pierced heart and, with the other, held out the Rosary as if it were the key to unlock the treasures of that Immaculate Heart. The children told how a brilliant light came forth from between the open hands. This light penetrated their souls. Their first instinct was to fall on their knees and make the prayers of adoration the angel had taught them.

This reaction may seem strange, but its significance becomes clear when Lucy explains how, in that light which flooded their whole being, they were given a sense of the presence of God. They also saw themselves reflected in the light, as in a mirror. Furthermore, they were given a deep sense of sin. What enormous theological implications in this simple vision: Divine presence, self-knowledge, understanding of sin. These are the secrets which are revealed to those who know how to use the Rosary as the key to the Immaculate Heart of Mary. As we begin to pray it, we might place ourselves in the presence of Our Lady and ask her, the Seat of Wisdom, to open her hands and allow the light of which she is guardian to fill and flood our souls. Not surprisingly, one of the classic books on Fatima is entitled *Our Lady of Light.*

The panorama of Knock

I write of the panorama of Knock, because of the wide-angle vision that took place in the year 1879, on that windswept hill of Mary in the West of Ireland.

I will never forget the day when Mrs Coyne, one of the

prime patrons and promoters of Knock, took me by the arm and, standing in front of the gable wall of the old church, explained something of the many-splendoured vision which unfolded before the eyes of the witnesses on that dark rainy August night.

At Knock, Our Lady did not come alone. She came in the company of St Joseph and St John the Evangelist, and central to everything was the Lamb standing on the altar. We do not kneel before Mary in isolation from her Son. She does not stand high up in the cleft of a rock as at Lourdes, or hovering over an oak tree as at Fatima. At Knock, there is no secret niche or private chapel. She comes in the full splendour of the Supper of the Lamb and with her spouse, the Protector of the Church, and with the theologian-preacher, St John. The question raised at Vatican II, a century later, is aptly dealt with here, in this Mayo University of the Spirit. Mary appears in the full context of the Church and of the mystery of Christ. It is clear that she enjoys a special role, for she stands tall and resplendent, wearing a crown, but at the same time, is in a position of relatedness to the central figure of the Lamb.

Here at this shrine, more than anywhere else I can think of, the Eucharist and the Marian devotion take on a wholesome Christian flavour. St Joseph appears as a praying figure. St John, with the book and with his finger raised, takes the stance of a preacher. This compact gathering to the side of the altar conveys the idea of a liturgy of the word and, far from being a distraction from the central figure of the Lamb, they come across as the perfect lead-in to the Eucharistic mystery. Little wonder that Knock is considered a shrine of the Eucharist.

We must not see a contradiction between Mary and the Eucharist as might appear from an instruction that came from Rome around the time of the Council: Only prayers addressed to the Most Holy Trinity or to the Lord Jesus are to be said

before the Blessed Sacrament exposed. The result of this
decree, was, that when the Rosary was being said, the Blessed
Sacrament would be put away, or a veil placed over the
monstrance. I always thought the arrangement crude and
simplistic, and asked Fr Hilary Carpenter, the English
Dominican Assistant General, what the practice in Santa
Sabina was. He gave the delightful reply that 'we continue in
the tradition which has been ours for centuries: the
Dominican understanding of the Rosary, is that it is a Jesus-
centred, Bible-based prayer. It is not addressed to Mary as
such, but rather is a contemplation of the mysteries of the
sacred humanity made in the company of prayer. So it is an
ideal prayer for a time of exposition of the Blessed Sacrament.'

From the Rosary to Holy Communion
In *La Vie Spirituelle* (April 1941) Fr M. J. Nicolas has written
of a holy religious, Fr Vayssière, who died as Provincial of the
Dominicans at Toulouse:

> The grace of intimacy with Mary that he received, he
> owed first of all to the state of littleness to which he had
> been reduced and to which he had consented. But he
> owed it as well to his Rosary. During the long days of
> solitude at Sainte-Baume, he had acquired the habit of
> saying several Rosaries in the day, sometimes as many as
> six. He often said the whole of it kneeling. And it was not
> a mechanical and superficial recitation: his whole soul
> went into it, he delighted in it, he devoured it, he was
> persuaded that he found in it, all that one could seek for
> in prayer. 'Recite each decade', he used to say, 'less
> reflecting on the mystery than communicating through
> the heart in its grace, and in the spirit of Jesus and Mary
> as the mystery presents it to us. The Rosary is the evening

Communion (elsewhere he calls it the Communion of the whole day) and it translates into light and fruitful resolutions the morning Communion. It is not merely a series of Ave Marias piously recited; it is Jesus living again in the soul through Mary's maternal action.

Thus he lived in the perpetually moving cycle of his Rosary, as if 'surrounded' by Christ and by Mary, communicating, as he said, in each of their states, in each aspect of their grace, entering thus into and remaining in the depth of God's heart: 'The Rosary is a chain of love from Mary to the Trinity.' One can understand what a contemplation it had become for him, what a way to pure union with God, what a need, like to that of Communion.

This Dominican spirituality finds itself at home saying the Rosary at Knock. Kneeling before the panorama at the gable wall of this shrine, both the Eucharist and the Rosary fall sweetly into place. Here, it becomes meaningful to say 'Hail Mary... the Lord is with you... and blessed is the fruit of your womb, Jesus.' No longer is there confusion between calling on Mary and looking at Jesus. In this vision they stand together. The vocal prayers and the contemplation of the mysteries harmonise in the figure of the Lamb standing beside his mother.

I can understand the inscription over the Rosary altar in Lourdes: To Jesus through Mary. But I identify more with the many-splendoured vision of Knock. Here, I want to take out my beads, lay them beside my New Testament and reach out directly to Jesus, in the company of Mary.

DEALING WITH DISTRACTIONS

Meditation on the mysteries can be blissfully simple, though indeed some people worry about their degree of attention or the extent of distractions. There are many answers to these problems, but the main thing is to ensure that we have committed ourselves to Jesus and made him Lord of our lives. Once that is so, then everything that concerns us is his concern too. Nothing is a distraction to God, so why should anything authentically human be a roadblock for us?

My own quaint way

My own quaint way of handling the situation arises out of the historical and philosophical background to the Rosary which cries aloud that all things in creation are good, and from God. Kept in right order, they are part and parcel of the total relationship of the creature, with him who is the Creator of all things, visible and invisible. With the priest at Mass I say: 'Blessed are you, Lord God of all creation. Through your goodness we have these gifts of bread and wine, of clothing and furniture, of work and play, of comings and goings, et cetera, all for your glory and our good.'

I tell the Lord that I rejoice in every detail of this world around me and especially in the wonder of my own being. I tell Jesus and Mary that I love them, and accept that they love me too and want to know everything about me. My day to day living is not sectioned off into a sacred section and a secular section. I don't believe in that crazy notion of a God-slot. It's like saying 'There's no God in Russia.' How do you keep him out? I don't come with any artificial holy make-up, specially put on for coming to church or prayer meeting. God is my Forever Friend with whom I live, twenty-four hours of the day, waking and sleeping, working and playing.

I don't want to be a split personality with one half of me belonging to God and the other half to the world or to myself. No, the whole caboodle is His. Pope John Paul uses the expression 'entrustment', which I believe conveys this sense of total abandonment. For Alan de la Roche and St Louis Marie de Montfort, this is the basic element in Rosary Confraternity commitment, which begins with a total consecration to Jesus and Mary.

Living in this all-round wholesome abandonment, it becomes hard to know what really is a distraction. God is more interested in my job, my finances, my relationships, in the love and the laughter that fills my day, than I could ever be. And I cannot, at a given holy time, switch off being me, and I certainly don't want to bring some fake me or some half me into prayer. So when that earthly side of me presents itself, there's no need to get steamed up and worried that I'm not praying. I hand everything over to God and come to him just as I am.

However, I must not let fussy detail or irrelevant circumstances so overwhelm me that they come between me and the Lord of life. Once I was brought to a woman who was ill and needed prayer. She received me kindly and we sat together for a long time, sometimes praying for healing, but most of the time just staying silent. I remembered the famous phrase: 'I call no man my friend until he can sit with me in silence.'

A week later I returned to find the patient well and with a lovely afternoon tea ready. As we sat and chatted, she remarked: 'I hope you did not think it rude of me not to have offered you something last time you were here. It was simply that I did not want anything to come between us and Jesus. I thought of Martha fussing with the dinner while Mary sat at the Master's feet and listened. I didn't want to be busy about many things, when only one thing was necessary.' Maybe that adds a necessary caution to my quaint treatment of distractions. They become such when I let them disturb the primacy of my intimate relationship with the person of the Lord.

Making the mysteries mine

One of the greatest helps towards settling down the wandering mind when saying the Rosary is to make the mysteries our own. At the mystery of the Annunciation for instance, we might ponder the fact that we each have our own annunciation. Each of us has a distinctive call, a life to live and work to do. So why should not this engage me during the Rosary?

My own practice on awakening in the morning is to reach for the beads and ask the Holy Spirit to enlighten me as to what this day holds. I pray that I may not miss the Lord's announcement, and fail to see the door of opportunity that awaits me.

In my pain and disappointment, in the things that trouble me, in my own agony and anger, I press my wounds to the glorious wounds of Jesus. I try to have the courage of President John F. Kennedy who prayed that he might be part of the agony of his times.

The Glorious mysteries might seem so totally remote as to be open to every distraction. But then I remember how Jesus said: 'I go to my Father and to your Father. I go to prepare a place for you, so that where I am, you also may be.' What could be more personal and guaranteed to hold my attention than that?

As for the Assumption and Coronation of Our Lady, we have only to remember that Mary is in heaven, body and soul. She is no disembodied spirit, but a total woman, alive in the fullness of her womanly personality. The things of the body and of this earth are very much her concern. The things we eat and drink, the work we do, the money we earn, the whole range of our human sexuality and our relationships, whether we are celibate or married – the Mother of God, bodily assumed into heaven, is not beyond this scene. As I ponder the mystery of this woman, now in glory yet totally human, I have no need to abstract from my own human situation. I think of a certain woman who prays every day that she may wear the right dress for the occasion, who presents to the Lord the carrots and potatoes, the bread and the milk, before placing them on the cooker and the dinner table. She has no problem, if in the midst of her prayer her mind turns occasionally to the meat in the oven. Her whole life is already God-soaked and committed to the Lordship of Jesus.

Well, that's my quaint way of dealing with distractions. But please don't think that it is easy or that I always succeed. A teacher who knew how to hold the attention of his pupils, and curb their wandering young minds and active imaginations, applied his secret to the matter of distraction in prayer. He would say 'that attention is co-extensive with interest and involvement.' So, in the Rosary, try to make the mysteries personal and practical. The following prayer may help to illustrate the point.

O Mary, mother of the Church, we come,
in union with your servant, Dominic,
to receive the gift of your Holy Rosary.
Teach us to accept God's will in the spirit of the Annunciation.
Visit us in our need, as you visited Elizabeth.
Bring us forth in grace, as you brought forth Jesus in the flesh.
Present us in the temple of the Father.
And help us to find Jesus in everyone we meet.

In our agony, may we say with Jesus: 'Father, your will be done.'
Grant that 'through his wounds we may be healed'.
Teach us the meekness of our king crowned with thorns.
Enable us to carry our cross with patience.
And obtain for us the grace of a happy and holy death.

May we 'know the power of his resurrection'
And ascend to that home prepared for us.
Grant that we may share in the fullness of the Holy Spirit,
And after this life, share in the glory of your Assumption
And Coronation as Queen of heaven.

Recent Popes Reflect on the Rosary

POPE JOHN XXIII
Apostolic Letter, 29 September 1961

It is true that some people who were not taught to pray other than as lip-service will recite the Rosary as a series of monotonous prayers, the Our Father, the Hail Mary, and the Gloria, arranged in the traditional set of fifteen decades. Without doubt, even this recitation is of some value. But, and we must stress this, it is only a beginning, an external ritual of confident prayer rather than an uplifting of the spirit to communion with God, whom we seek in the sublimity and tenderness of his mysteries, in his merciful love for all humanity.

The true substance of the Rosary, if it is meditated upon, lies in three relevant acts which give unity and coherence to the saying of it; that is, mystical contemplation, intimate reflection and good intention.

Mystical contemplation

First, the contemplation of each mystery, of those truths of faith which describe the redemptive mission of Christ. Through contemplation we can get closer in feeling and thought to the teaching and life of Jesus, the Son of God and the Son of Mary, who lived on earth to redeem, to instruct, to sanctify, in the silence of his hidden life of prayer and hard work, in the pain of his blessed passion, in the triumph of his resurrection, just as in the glory of the heavens, where he sits at the right hand of God the Father, ready always to help and to quicken, through the Holy Spirit, the Church founded by him and advancing in his path through the centuries.

Intimate reflection

The second act is to reflect; reflection fills the soul of the person who prays with the light of Christ's mysteries. We can all find in those mysteries an example to make our own, related to the condition in which we live. Enlightened by the Holy Spirit, who, from the depths of the soul in grace 'intercedes for us with sighs too deep for words' (Romans 8), we can face our existence with the renewal that springs from those mysteries, and we can find endless applications to our spiritual needs, as well as to our daily life.

Good intention

The last act is intention; that is, to name the persons, the social and personal needs that represent, for the person praying, an exercise of charity towards his fellows, the charity that is the living expression of communion in the Mystical Body of Christ.

In this way the Rosary becomes a universal plea, from individuals and from the immense community of the faithful which is united by this single prayer, whether it be for personal intentions, or personal gratitude, or as part of the unanimous voice of the Church for the intentions of all humanity. As the Redeemer himself willed it, the Church lives amid contention, adversity and opposition, which often become a frightening threat, but she looks forward, undaunted, to her final home.

Spoken and private recitation

Vocal prayers have their own importance. The Rosary takes on beauty from the reciter: the innocent child, the sick person, the parents urged on by their great sense of responsibility, the modest families who are faithful to the old traditions of the home where the Rosary is said with confidence, aloud or in silence, amid a life of uncertainties and temptations.

Praying solemnly together

In paying respect to this old, time-honoured and moving form of devotion, we take note of the many changes of modern life that have had their effect even on the functions and forms of Christian prayer. Now the person who prays does not feel alone any more but feels more than ever that he belongs to a society sharing the responsibilities, enjoying the advantages, and facing the same uncertainties and dangers. This is, besides, the character of the liturgical prayer, contained in the Missal and breviary. At the beginning of each prayer marked by the words 'Let us pray…' there is pre-supposed the sense of community not only of the priest who is praying, but also of the person or persons for whose intentions the prayer is being offered. The multitude is praying as one single supplicating voice for brotherhood in everything man does. The Rosary is a means at hand for praying, publicly and universally, for the sake of the ordinary and extraordinary needs of mankind and the world.

POPE PAUL VI

According to Pope Paul VI the Rosary has been called 'the compendium of the entire Gospel'.

Our interest in the Rosary has led us to follow very attentively the numerous meetings which in recent years have been devoted to the pastoral role of the Rosary in the modern world, meetings arranged by associations and individuals profoundly attached to the Rosary and attended by bishops, priests, religious and lay people of proven experience and recognised ecclesial awareness.

Among these people, special mention should be made of the sons of St Dominic, by tradition the guardians and promoters of this very salutary practice. Parallel with such meetings has been the research work of historians, work aimed not at defining in a sort of archaeological fashion the primitive form of the Rosary but at uncovering the original inspiration and driving force behind it and its essential structure. The fundamental characteristics of the Rosary, its essential elements and their mutual relationship have all emerged more clearly from these congresses and from the search carried out.

The Gospel inspiration

Thus, for instance, the Gospel inspiration of the Rosary has appeared more clearly: the Rosary draws from the Gospel the presentation of the mysteries and its main formulas. As it moves from the Angel's joyful greeting and the Virgin's pious assent, the Rosary takes its inspiration from the Gospel to suggest the attitude with which the faithful should recite it.

In the harmonious succession of Hail Marys the Rosary puts before us once more a fundamental mystery of the Gospel: the Incarnation of the Word, contemplated at the decisive moment of the Annunciation to Mary. The Rosary is thus a Gospel prayer, as pastors and scholars like to define it, more today, perhaps, than in the past.

A Christ-centred prayer

As a Gospel prayer, centred on the mystery of the redemptive Incarnation, the Rosary is a prayer with a clearly Christological orientation. Its most characteristic element, in fact, the litany-like succession of Hail Marys, becomes in itself an unceasing praise of Christ, who is the ultimate object both of the Angel's announcement and of the greeting of the Mother of John the Baptist: 'Blessed is the fruit of your womb' (Luke 1: 42).

We would go further and say that the succession of Hail Marys constitutes the warp on which is woven the contemplation of the mysteries. The Jesus that each Hail Mary recalls is the same Jesus whom the succession of the mysteries proposes to us – now as the Son of God, now as the Son of the Virgin – at his birth in a stable at Bethlehem, at his presentation by his Mother in the temple, as a youth full of zeal for his Father's affairs, as the Redeemer in agony in the garden, scourged and crowned with thorns, carrying the Cross and dying on Calvary; risen from the dead and ascended to the glory of the Father to send forth the gift of the Spirit.

The Jesus phrases

As is well known, at one time there was a custom, still preserved in certain places, of adding to the name of Jesus in each Hail Mary a reference to the mystery being contemplated. And this was done precisely in order to help contemplation and to make the mind and the voice act in unison.

There has also been felt with greater urgency the need to point out once more the importance of a further essential element in the Rosary, in addition to the value of the elements of praise and petition, namely, the element of contemplation. Without this the Rosary is a body without a soul, and its recitation is in danger of becoming a mechanical repetition of formulas and of going counter to the warning of Christ: 'And in praying do not heap up empty phrases as the Gentiles do; for they think that they will be heard for their many words.' (Mt 6:7).

Quiet rhythm

By its nature the recitation of the Rosary calls for a quiet rhythm and a lingering pace, helping the individual to meditate on the mysteries of the Lord's life as seen through the eyes of her who was closest to the Lord. In this way the unfathomable riches of these mysteries are unfolded.

And the liturgy

Finally, as a result of modern reflection the relationships between the liturgy and the Rosary have been more clearly understood. On the one hand it has been emphasised that the Rosary is, as it were, a branch sprung from the ancient trunk of the Christian liturgy, the Psalter of the Blessed Virgin whereby the humble were associated in the Church's hymn of praise and universal intercession.

The Rosary is an exercise of piety that draws its motivating force from the liturgy and leads naturally back to it, if practised in conformity with its original inspiration. It does not, however, become part of the liturgy. In fact, meditation on the mysteries of the Rosary, by familiarising the hearts and minds of the faithful with the mysteries of Christ, can be an excellent preparation for the celebration of those same mysteries in the liturgical action and can also become a continuing echo thereof.

Scripture, song and silence

In recent times certain exercises of piety have been created which take their inspiration from the Rosary. Among such exercises we wish to draw attention to and recommend those which insert into the ordinary celebration of the Word of God some elements of the Rosary, such as meditation on the mysteries and the litany-like repetition of the angel's greeting to Mary. In this way these elements gain in importance, since they are found in the context of Bible readings, illustrated with a homily, accompanied by silent pauses and emphasised with song. We are happy to know that such practices have helped to promote a more complete understanding of the spiritual riches of the Rosary itself and have served to restore esteem for its recitation among youth.

Communal prayer – vital to the family

We now desire, as a continuation of the thought of our predecessors, to recommend strongly the recitation of the family Rosary. Vatican II has pointed out how the family, the primary and vital cell of society, 'shows itself to be the domestic sanctuary of the Church through the mutual affection of its members and the common prayer they offer to God'.

The Christian family is thus seen to be a domestic Church if its members, each according to his proper place and tasks, all together promote justice, practise works of mercy, devote themselves to helping their brethren, take part in the apostolate of the wider local community and play their part in its liturgical worship. This will be all the more true if together they offer up prayers to God. If this element of common prayer were missing, the family would lack its very character as a domestic Church. Thus there must logically follow a concrete effort to reinstate communal prayer in family life if there is to be a restoration of the theological concept of the family as the domestic Church.

The family Rosary – no effort to be spared

But there is no doubt that, after the celebration of the Liturgy of the Hours, the high point which family prayer can reach, the Rosary should be considered as one of the best and most efficacious prayers in common that the Christian family is invited to recite. We like to think, and sincerely hope, that when the family gathering becomes a time of prayer the Rosary is a frequent and favoured manner of praying.

We are well aware that the changed conditions of life today do not make family gatherings easy, and that even when such a gathering is possible many circumstances make it difficult to turn it into an occasion of prayer. There is no doubt of the difficulty. But it is characteristic of the Christian in his manner of life not to give in to circumstances but to overcome them, not to succumb but to make an effort. Families which want to live in full measure the vocation and spirituality proper to the Christian family must therefore devote all their energies to overcoming the pressures that hinder family gatherings and prayer in common.

Serenely free – intrinsic appeal

In concluding these observations, which give proof of the concern and esteem which the Apostolic See has for the Rosary of the Blessed Virgin, we desire at the same time to recommend that this very worthy devotion should not be propagated in a way that is too one-sided or exclusive. The Rosary is an excellent prayer, but the faithful should feel serenely free in its regard. They should be drawn to its calm recitation by its intrinsic appeal.

POPE JOHN PAUL II

The recitation of the Rosary is a prayer which is both simple and profound; it is at the same time Christ-centred, Marian, and directed towards the whole people of God (Christological, Mariological and ecclesial).

Only in this perspective does it show the reason for its existence, its work, its aim and the criteria for its way of proceeding. Everything is in the light of Christ, Mary and the Church. In the Rosary we contemplate the mysteries of Christ through the eyes of Mary. It is she who reveals them to us, helps us to appreciate them, brings them within our grasp, 'scales them down' to our littleness and weakness. Mary is, at the same time the spokesperson for all humanity in the presence of her Son, for the humanity which suffers and is oppressed, in searching for truth and salvation.

Mary is at the summit of the people of God, to intercede for all the faithful who are its members.

The mystery of Mary is rich in possibilities that make for an understanding of the lay charism. The Rosary is one of the most meaningful prayers for the faithful of every age and every condition. In the Rosary, even the most lowly and humble son or daughter of the people of God can find the fullness of his or her baptismal vocation, his or her prophetic, priestly and kingly role, and can find, in and through Mary, an extraordinary capacity to approach the heart of Christ and of the Father.

In the Rosary, Mary herself gathers up the prayers of the poor and humble and clothes them with a most potent ability to intercede before the throne of the Most High.

The Rosary, thanks to Mary, brings the saving light of the mysteries of Christ to shine on all the circumstances and difficulties of our daily life, work, labours, doubts, suffering, family and social lives, and transforms it all, raises it up and purifies it. It is a prayer that springs from an awareness of the maternal role of Mary, who inspires and protects the Church.

The Rosary presents to us, against the background of the mysteries of Christ and Mary, those events which are common in the life of every Christian: the mysteries of joy and suffering and of glory; mysteries that speak of grace and virtue and sanctity. Our pastors must keep their eyes fixed on these things, for they constitute the basis of the dignity of the laity.

Thus, meditating with Mary, we contemplate in her life and in the life of her Son, the life of every Christian who is called amidst the transitory yet fascinating responsibilities of culture, family, society, politics and work, to possess a single criterion for all his activity, the very life of Christ and his word which are available to us, in complete truth, through the unbroken tradition of the Church and her magisterium.

This living word of God is continually inspiring new initiatives, through the passion of many thousands of men and women, to bring the values of the Gospel to the historical and temporal order of our world. They thus bring to maturity those fruits Jesus hoped for when he told his disciples:

> Go therefore and make disciples of all nations, baptising them in the name of the Father and of the Son and of the Holy Spirit, teaching them to observe all that I have commanded you. (Matthew 28:19:20)

Lifted up on the Cross, at the very moment when he seemed to be defeated, the Son of God spoke of a vocation, entrusted a mission:

> 'Woman, behold your son…'
> 'Behold, your Mother!' (John 19:26:27)

Mary not only goes before us in that total 'yes' to God, but she also teaches us to make that 'yes' our own in the circumstances in which each one of us is called to live. The courage of her obedience, her gaze always directed towards Christ, her life radically turned towards God, the boldness of her initiatives, of charity for Elizabeth, at the marriage of Cana, during the public ministry of her Son, at the foot of the cross, in the Upper Room, all these are different examples of Mary the Mother of the vocation and mission of every Christian.

This fact gives us great hope. In my apostolic journeys I have met new lay groups, new movements and associations, ever greater numbers of young people and adults who are discovering in the living Christ the reason for their hope and their joy. I cannot then but think of the intercession of Mary who continually obtains from her Son new graces for us all

My favourite prayer – so rich, so simple

The Rosary is my favourite prayer. A marvellous prayer! Marvellous in its simplicity and in its depth. In this prayer we repeat many times the words that the Virgin Mary heard from the Archangel, and from her kinswoman Elizabeth. The whole Church joins in these words. It can be said that the Rosary is, in a certain way, a prayer-commentary on the last chapter of the constitution *Lumen gentium* of Vatican II, a chapter which deals with the wonderful presence of the Mother of God in the mystery of Christ and the Church.

In fact, against the background of the words 'Ave Maria' there passes before the eyes of the soul the main episodes in the life of Jesus Christ. They are composed of the joyful, sorrowful and glorious mysteries and they put us in living communion with Jesus through, we could say, his Mother's heart.

At the same time our heart can enclose in these decades of the Rosary all the facts that make up the life of the individual, the family, the nation, the Church and mankind. Personal matters and those of our neighbour, and particularly of those who are closest to us, who are dearest to us. Thus the simple prayer of the Rosary beats the rhythm of human life.

THE ECUMENICAL BRIDGES
OF THE BEADS

God be with the days when I would fly from Dublin to the Isle of Man every Sunday morning at the invitation of that wonderful parish priest, Fr McGrath. It was holiday season and several Protestants, Jews and Muslims would turn up at the open-air Mass in the magnificent Lourdes shrine alongside the church. To my amazement, they showed a keen interest in the story of the beautiful Lady who had appeared in the Grotto of Massabielle. We told them how she wore a golden rose on each foot and had a golden Rosary chain over her arm.

Fr McGrath would speak in loving terms of Mary who smiled on Bernadette, and tell everyone that she was still smiling on them too. My own role was to speak about the Rosary and invite the Protestants and the others to accept the present of a blessed beads. I would offer copies of the New Testament to the Catholics, and encourage them to use it, for the purpose of deepening their understanding of the Rosary mysteries. The theme of the Bible and the Beads helped build many ecumenical bridges.

Pope Paul VI referred to the Anglicans whose classical theologians have drawn attention to the sound scriptural basis for devotion to the Mother of Our Lord, and have underlined the importance of Mary's place in the Christian life. He points out that 'any manifestation of piety which is opposed to correct practice should be eliminated, and every care must be exercised to avoid exaggerations which could mislead other Christian brethren'. True devotion to Christ must be 'an approach to Christ, the source and centre of ecclesiastical communion, in which all who confess that Jesus is God and

Lord, Saviour and sole Mediator, are called to be one, with each other, with Christ, and with the Father in the unity of the Holy Spirit' (*Marialis cultus* 32).

As far back as 1948, Fr Wilfred Jukka, a Montfort priest, was writing:

> You can't shock a New Yorker.... Yet I imagine that even they got a shock, when they read how a leading Methodist there had been urging Protestants to say the Rosary. He was telling college students that Protestant prayer lacked a system of controlled meditation, and he advised his co-religionists to seize upon the possibilities it offered towards uniting souls with Christ.

Richard Baumann

The testimony of Richard Baumann, minister of the Evangelical Church of Württemberg, is striking:

> When the Rosary is said, truth sinks into the subconscious like a slow and steady downpour.... It is a long and persevering gaze, a meditation, a quieting of the spirit in the praise of God, the value of which we Protestants are learning once more. In this chain of love, the cross is the dominant symbol, the beads being a prop for the memory, a help against impatience, so that a set length of time may be adhered to.

Gerard Irvine

The Reverend Gerard Irvine, an Anglican clergyman in London, gives the following testimony:

> I am a cradle member of the Church of England and all my life I have used the Rosary. On my father's side I am

of Ulster Protestant stock. I was taken every morning to the Anglican Eucharist and, during the service, I was given a Rosary by my mother. I was told to think of as many terms of endearment for Jesus as I could, while passing the beads through my fingers. So I grew up with the idea of a Rosary as an accompaniment to prayer.

At the same time, I was taught to love and trust Our Lady, and to ask her prayers, but it was not until my teens that I put the use of the Rosary and the Hail Mary together. After discovering an Anglican book with instructions on the mysteries, I set myself to use the Rosary in the traditional Catholic way. At college in Oxford, I was a pupil of that great saint and scholar, Austin Farrer, who in one of his books describes the Rosary as a heaven-sent aid.

The set of beads I have been using for the last fifteen years is very precious to me. What makes it particularly valuable, is it was blessed for me by Pope John, the twenty-third. I hope that when the time comes, it may accompany me into the coffin. But much more, I hope that the Mother whose prayers I invoke, when I say the Rosary, will then show me the blessed fruit of her womb, Jesus.

Neville Ward

Neville Ward, in his delightful book *Five for Sorrow, Ten for Joy*, mentions that in Methodism the silence about the Mother of Jesus is positively deafening and wonders about this surprising mental hang-up. 'But,' he says, 'I am beginning to discover among my people, signs of shy but nervous interest in her mysterious being.'

Geoffrey Bacon

Not so long ago, I had the privilege of conducting a Rosary weekend at Suzy and Peter Seed's retreat centre in Scotland, where I came across a wonderful Presbyterian minister, Geoffrey Bacon, and his deaconess wife. They had come with a number of their parishioners to join us, and what a blessing they proved to be. They all had their beads, as did their minister, who gave us the fruit of his own profound Rosary meditations. The slow, deliberate manner in which they said the vocal prayers was an inspiration.

Robert Llewelyn

But what thrilled me most of all was when they issued an invitation to the rest of us to come to their own parish for a Rosary day of prayer. They had as guest speaker that wonderful retired Anglican priest Robert Llewelyn. He had been chaplain to the Julian Shrine at Norwich from 1976 to 1990. He spoke to a denominationally mixed audience for three hours on the Rosary as a prayer which brings healing and rest.

Never have I listened to more beautiful and sound practical teaching on the Rosary. I will carry with me to the grave the sight of that gracious gentleman of God as he lovingly handled the beads and led us through his own book, *A Doorway to Silence,* into a garden of loveliness, peace, and healing. Incidentally, after each decade, Fr Robert prayed the very invocation from *The Healing Light of the Rosary,* so widely used in Roman Catholic circles. As a mark of common interest and sincere friendship, he gave me a copy of his book with a personal inscription which I will always cherish.

'I'm now eighty-three', he said, 'and only at the age of seventy-five did I get drawn into the Rosary. I find it a bridge to contemplative prayer. The Rosary meets us wherever we are in the ways of prayer. It brings peace and serenity and is eminently suited for healing. The tortured mind can cling to it.'

The words Hail, blessed, now, death, resonate peace.

We know the value of sight and sound as aids to prayer. We must discover the sense of touch. The beads are something to reach out to. Touch brings awareness; it stills the racing brain.

We need not fear addressing Mary as Blessed. This is simply the fulfilling of prophecy, that all generations would call to her so. We know indeed that God is merciful, but there is a gut thing that makes us run to our Mother.

We do not pray for sinners down there, we ourselves are the sinners. We say: pray for *us,* sinners.

We don't work on the words, it is the words that work on us. They work on a subconscious level. The words are like the banks of a river. The mystery is the river itself. As this river of life flows out into the sea, the banks fall away, and we are lost in the ocean of God himself.

Don't be worried about the repetition. What Jesus condemned was vain repetition. Hitting a nail over and over again is repetition, but each time the nail is being driven deeper into the wood. So does our prayer reach deeper into the heart of God.

Distractions can become a source of healing if we know how to handle them. Something that occurs over and over again may indicate a situation which needs to be confronted and dealt with.

We may begin with a prayer that is saying a prayer. We have to become a prayer. Our whole life must become a prayer. However, we will never learn to pray all the time, unless we learn to pray some of the time.

Love alone validates our prayer.

John Henning
John is a convert to Catholicism, and the following piece by
him appeared in *The Rosary Letter:*

It happened some time ago, in one of Dublin's main
streets. Taking her hankie our of her handbag, a girl
dropped her beads on the pavement. A Protestant
clergyman passing picked them up, and handing them
back to the girl said: 'There you are, oh excuse me,
would you mind telling me how you work this thing?'
Since I became a Catholic, I have often wondered,
do Catholics realise what a difference it makes whether
you know how to 'work this thing' or not? In these
countries and on the Continent, the use of the beads
was, and still is, regarded as the characteristic of the
Catholic. Reading the special form 'for reconciling
converted Papists for our Church' which, from 1700 to
1730 was used in the Church of Ireland, I noticed that
one of the first things which the apostate was made to
say was: 'I will lay aside my beads and Ave Marias.'
My father was a schoolteacher in Luther's home
country. The main subject he had to teach was religious
knowledge. He regarded it as one of his principal duties
to inspire his pupils not only with respect of other
creeds, but also with a certain knowledge of their tenets
and practices.
For this purpose he had a collection of religious and
devotional objects, and there was hardly a greater treat
he could give us on a Sunday afternoon than to afford us
a 'private show' of this collection. There was a Jewish
teffiloth (or prayer-belt), an ivory statue of Buddha, a
Tibetan prayer mill, a piece of polished wood bearing
the inscription 'Gethsemane' (my grandfather had

114

brought it home from his tour of the Holy Land), a piece of brimstone from the shore of the Dead Sea, and there was also a Rosary. My father used to convey to us some of the horror he had experienced when buying this 'object' in the little dusty store of 'repository art' behind 'the' Catholic church of our town (which incidentally numbered some 600,000 inhabitants).

While explaining to us the curious way of working the beads, he would allow us to slip the black beads through our fingers.

So, that was what Catholicism felt like!

Sometimes when in Church I hear that mysterious clicking noise of a Rosary 'being worked', I am overcome again by that feeling of utter strangeness.

How far away I strayed from the tradition of my ancestors who were all Protestant clergymen and schoolmasters, I never realised more clearly than when, after my reception into the Church, my sister visiting my house one day discovered my beads on my bedside table, and holding them up by the tips of her fingers she exclaimed: 'Well I never!' It was so strange.

I was then living in a district predominantly Catholic. Everybody, especially the workmen in my factory, regarded me as a member of the small group of Protestant 'planters'. One day our chauffeur had the misfortune of knocking down a child who ran into his car and was killed immediately. I accompanied our chauffeur to the police-barracks where he was to be questioned. He was a sturdy boorish type of man, and it was an awful experience while we were waiting for the police-inspector, to have him sitting there beside me, shivering and crying like a child. Eventually I took my beads out of my pocket, and putting them between his clasped fingers, I said to him: 'Now look here, you know as well as I do, that it was not your fault. Keep your wits together, and say a prayer for the child and her mother. More we cannot do just now.' I shall never forget the change in that man. The moment he felt the beads between his fingers, he was able to control himself, and quietly moving his lips to the venerable words, he regained peace.

During the war, it happened that Catholics of different nations recognised one another by their Rosary beads. I still remember the first night I was in Ireland. Sitting by the fire in my first 'digs' I could not help feeling desperately lonely. Suddenly I heard a murmuring noise through the wall, coming at regular intervals. It took me some time to realise what it was but when I recognised that it was the family Rosary, I was overcome by a feeling of deep gratitude.

I felt at home.

MEDITATIONS

FOR PERSONAL AND GENERAL USE

THE FIVE JOYFUL MYSTERIES

The Annunciation
Let what you have said be done to me.

O God, I pray that I may be a door,
through which your word may enter.
Give me a mind open to your light.
Give me a heart ever open to your love.
I place myself in your hands,
that through me,
you may enter your own world,
as once you entered it
through the open door of Mary.

The Visitation
Who am I, that the mother of my Lord should visit me!

O Mary, the sound of your voice
filled Elizabeth with the Holy Spirit,
so that the child in her womb leapt for joy.
Let your voice sound now, in my ears,
so that I too, may be filled with the Spirit
and experience the joy which comes
from the Christ-child you carry.

The Nativity
To you is born a Saviour.

Come, Lord Jesus, to the inn of my soul.
Your birth is my birth,
creating and recreating me.
Come to the cavern of my heart.
that I may live anew,
that I may glow with love,
that I may know the glory
of new birth.
O Jesus, with the shepherds of Bethlehem
I welcome you as my Saviour.

The Presentation
They took the child to Jerusalem to present him to the Lord.

O Divine Weaver,
I present to you
the strands of my broken humanity
with all their ragged endings.
Run them through with the silver thread
of your divinity,
that your ways may be woven
into mine.
So, may I become
a presentation
acceptable in your sight.

The Finding in the Temple

They found him ... with the Jewish teachers, listening to them and asking questions.

O Jesus, you are
the wisdom of the ages
and the wonder of the world.
Come to the temple of my heart.
Sit with me,
as you sat with the teachers of Israel.
Search my heart with your questions
Listen to my foolish ways
and make me truly wise.

THE FIVE SORROWFUL MYSTERIES

The Agony in the Garden

Father, not what I want, but what you want.

Dear Jesus,
Gethsemane has grown wild and great,
and the chalice of life's sorrow
is the same, that would not pass you by.
May our agony be one with yours.
Through your pain and sorrow,
may we find courage
to walk together
through this garden of sorrow
to the splendours of Paradise.

The Scourging of Jesus
We are healed by the punishments he suffered, made whole by the scourges he received.

Lord, Jesus, wash us clean in the blood
that flowed from your sacred body,
as you were scourged for our sins.
By your precious and glorious wounds
heal us in body, soul and spirit.
In the hour of death,
when we stand before you,
with unclean and empty hands,
Have mercy on us and be our Saviour.

The Crowning with Thorns
Plaiting a crown of thorns, they put it on his head and mocked him.

Dear Lord,
you came as King,
but they crowned you as a fool.
They spat upon your face,
and mocked you.
We now enthrone you,
and acknowledge you as Lord
of all that we are, and all that we have.
King of glory, reign in our hearts.
We place ourselves in your hands
and pledge our love and loyalty.

The Carrying of the Cross
Come follow me…

Dear Lord,
you come bearing the burden
of our sin and sorrow.
You meet us
at the crossroads of Calvary.
Extend to us
the merits of your painful journey,
so that we may have the courage
to walk through the valley of darkness
along life's road to our home in heaven.

The Crucifixion
Into your hands I commend my spirit.

Lord, Jesus, I pray in this mystery
for the grace of a happy and holy death.
Death for you was no defeat,
but the final offering of your life.
May I so live,
that all my thoughts, words and actions,
may be an offering to God.
When the end comes,
may I breathe out my soul,
crying to the Father with you:
'Into your hands I commend my spirit.'

THE FIVE GLORIOUS MYSTERIES

The Resurrection

*If the Spirit of him who raised Jesus from the dead dwells in you,
then he who raised Jesus from the dead will give eternal life to your
perishable bodies too.*

Lord, we give thanks
for that word of assurance.
We claim its promise.
Give glory to our perishable bodies,
and clothe our frail flesh
with your own glorious immortality.
Dying you destroyed our death,
Rising you restored our life.
Lord Jesus, come in glory.

The Ascension

*God's mercy is so abundant, and his love so great, that he brought
us to life with Christ. In our union with Christ Jesus, he raised us
up with him to rule with him in the heavenly world.*

Father, we thank you
for your abundant mercy.
May we live,
no longer out of our own earthly ration,
but out of the heavenly supply of
your generous giving.
May we lift up our hearts
to share the throne
with Jesus your Son, who calls us
to rule and reign with him
in the heavenly world.

'To him who wins the victory,
I will give authority to share my throne.'

The Descent of the Holy Spirit
You send forth your spirit, Lord, and renew the face of the earth.

Spirit of the living God, fall afresh on us.
Light up the darkness of our ways.
Warm the coldness of our hearts.
Blow like a breath of spring over our lives
and renew the face of the earth.
You came on Mary,
so that Jesus would be born of her.
Come now on us,
so that through your power,
Jesus may be formed again,
the fruit of our life, our love and our labour.

The Assumption of Our Lady
We know that when this tent we live in, our body here on earth,
is torn down, God will have a house in heaven for us.

O Virgin Mother,
You have gone before us
on our pilgrim way.
You are the star that leads us home.
Do not cease to care for those,
struggling with difficulties,
with their lips pressed
to life's bitter cup of sorrow.
Have pity on those who weep,
on those who fear.
Grant hope and peace to all,

and after this our exile,
show unto us the
blessed fruit of your womb, Jesus

The Coronation of Our Lady

*A great sign appeared in heaven, a woman clothed with the sun,
the moon under her feet, and on her head a crown of twelve stars.*

Beloved Daughter of the Father,
First Lady of heaven,
Housekeeper of the Trinity,
Temple of the Holy Spirit,
Queen of the New Creation.
You are the Keeper of the King's secrets,
and you still treasure those secrets
in your Immaculate Heart.
O, Mary, Queen of all hearts,
the loving service that you gave
at Nazareth, at Cana and on Calvary
has not ended.
We look to you, Queen
and Mother of the Church.

FOR THE FAMILY

Before the family Rosary

Most Holy Trinity, Father, Son and Holy Spirit, we, the members of this family, place ourselves under your protection. Through the mysteries of the Rosary may we know your plan of salvation, and learn how much you love us. May your kingdom come in our family so that we may one day share in your heavenly home hereafter.

THE FIVE JOYFUL MYSTERIES

The Annunciation

The world's salvation begins with a mother and child. We offer this mystery for the mothers and children of the world and especially for our own.

When Mary heard the message of the angel she recognised God's will and opened her heart to receive it: 'Be it done unto me according to your word.'

Heavenly Father, make known your personal annunciation for each member of this family, and give us the grace to fulfil it as our life's vocation.

The Visitation

O Mary, your visit brought joy to the house of Elizabeth, and your voice brought grace to the child in her womb. Renew the wonder of your visitation in our home this night. Let your voice rejoice in our hearts and your smile light up the dark days of our lives.

The Nativity

O God, it is strange and wondrous that the world's salvation begins with a little child. In the Bible it is written: 'a little child shall lead them.' O little child of Bethlehem, lead all the members of this family to fall down before you in adoration. We cannot bring you sheep or lambs as the shepherds did; we cannot lay gold or silver or precious incense at your feet. But we bring you the treasures of our faith and we offer you our hearts as a cradle for your own life and love.

The Presentation in the Temple

We come now to present our family to you, God our Father. May it be a pleasing offering in your sight. May we always live united to you; never let us by thought, word or deed pierce the Immaculate Heart of our Mother.

Let our daily activities pass through the work-worn hands of St Joseph, and may the Infant Jesus be a light to our children to guide them to the final presentation in the realms of glory.

The Finding of Jesus in the Temple

What sorrow for Mary and Joseph to lose the most wonderful child in the world!

And what sorrow for so many parents who lose their children today – through death, or war, or misunderstanding, or through the simple fact that the time for parting has come.

O Divine Child, keep our family one. And however our paths may lead us, may we all direct our steps towards you, so that in finding you who are the end of all our searching, we may find each other.

THE SORROWFUL MYSTERIES

The Agony in the Garden

Every family has its hour of agony, its time of trial and tribulation. This is the dark hour when we must go to Gethsemane to find strength in the agony of Jesus. 'Being in an agony,' the Gospel says, 'he prayed the longer.'

Prayer is the great source of strength and consolation. Heavenly Father, when our lips are pressed against life's bitter cup of sorrow, may we have the courage to say with you: 'Father, not my will, but yours be done.'

Come what may, we will preserve our peace of mind, knowing that we are in the hands of a loving Father.

The Scourging at the Pillar

You were led, Lord, like a sheep to the slaughter and did not open your mouth. We have seen you as a leper, as it were, one struck by God and afflicted. It was for our sins you were struck down. By the cruel wounds inflicted on you, heal our spiritual and bodily illness.

Grant Lord, that every member of this family, may in this mystery, make reparation for the offences committed against your holy body, which is the Church.

The Crowning with Thorns

Dear Jesus, you came as King of love and mercy and they crowned you as a fool.

We, the members of this family, make reparation to your most Sacred Heart for the sins against authority: in the State, in the Church, and in family life.

May we reverence our parents and respect in them the God-given authority to rule by love and mercy the children committed to their care.

The Carrying of the Cross

Father and Mother have to shoulder many crosses. Parents have the joy of bringing children into the world, but they have to carry them for a long time before they stand on their own two feet. Children have their crosses too; they often suffer in silence and meet no Simon or Veronica on the way.

No wonder, Lord, that you said to the women of Jerusalem: 'Weep not for me, but weep for yourselves and for your children....'

Teach us in this mystery, Jesus, to realise that we do not carry the cross alone; we are a family and we carry each other. And you are out ahead of us and we walk in your footsteps.

The Crucifixion

Death will come, but it will never take our love away; for you, Lord, are our true love and our abiding hope.

To die is to go to a new and better home. And so, dear Lord, when the hour comes to be with you in Paradise, may we kiss the cross and say as you did: 'Father, into your hands, I commit my spirit.'

And may each one of us be able to say, as you did, when the end came: 'I have finished the work the Father gave me to do.'

THE GLORIOUS MYSTERIES

The Resurrection

In this mystery, Lord, we are filled with the hope that our family and friends will rise from the grave and share in the triumph of your resurrection.

By the power of these sacred Rosary mysteries we know that the bodies we have cared for with such loving attention will rise in glory to share in the wonders of the new life that will never end.

When crushed beneath our burdens may we recall this blessed mystery of rising up, and come face to face with you, our steadfast risen Saviour.

The Ascension

As we gather in this earthly home, Lord, we can do no better than linger over the loving promise you made on the night before you died:

'There are many dwellings in my Father's house;
I am going there to prepare a place for you...'

Dear Jesus, when the time comes to bid farewell to this home and family, may we set out with the Rosary still in our hands, as the key to the door of heaven.

The Descent of the Holy Spirit

Heavenly Father, send your Holy Spirit on the father of this family that he may preside over it with true wisdom and loving care.

O Mary, noble Bride of the Spirit, give to our mother the gifts of understanding and counsel, that she may have a heart ready to listen and to lead.

Give to our children eyes for the unseen; ears open to the prompting of the Spirit and hearts filled with fortitude.

O Holy Spirit, may your coming to this home be a renewal of the grace of Pentecost.

The Assumption of Mary

Dear Mother, you are now in heaven, body and soul, to tell us that salvation is not for souls only, but for human beings in their many-splendoured glory.

Lord, we thank you for the bodily powers you have given us. Everything human and bodily is wonderful and nothing truly human will ever be lost. As we contemplate Mary's bodily

Assumption, we find new strength to labour for our daily bread, to feed and clothe our children, to serve the sick and comfort the lonely.

May our family play its part in building up this earthly creation, so that we may merit to share body and soul in the glory to come.

The Coronation

Since you are Queen, Mother, you must reign. We acknowledge you as Queen of this family. We salute you as the First Lady of this home. Hail Mary, full of grace, the Lord is with you; hail our life, our sweetness and our hope.

But how can you reign, O gracious Lady, unless you have servants at your command? And so, we ask you to reveal to us your wishes, so that every member of this family may have the honour of being in your royal service.

After the family Rosary

Holy Mary, Mother of God, be a mother to each one in this home. As in Cana you watched over the needs of a married couple, watch now over the needs of this family. And as you stood by the cross of your Son and saw him die, stand by each one of us, father, mother, children, and lead us at the hour of death to our true home in heaven.

BEFORE MASS OR IN THE PRESENCE OF THE BLESSED SACRAMENT

THE JOYFUL MYSTERIES

The Annunciation
O Jesus! I adore you, hidden in this divine sacrament, as I adore you hidden in the precious womb of the Blessed Virgin. Lord, I am not worthy to receive you.

Come, Holy Spirit, upon me, as you came upon Mary, so that I may be open to receive Jesus, as she did on the day of the Annunciation.

The Visitation
O Mary, your visit brought joy to Elizabeth, grace to the infant John, and healing to Zachary. Your womb was the first tabernacle for the Bread come down from heaven. Through this Holy Communion with your Son, bring us joy and grace and healing for soul and body.

The Nativity
I adore you, O Word made flesh. I adore you, true God, clothed in our humanity and sharing our weakness and our wounds. May this Holy Communion be, for us, a share in the sacred birth by which all things are made new.

The Presentation
Mother Mary, you offered your Son to the Eternal Father for the sins of the world; grant that I may never wander from the home of my heavenly Father. Through this Holy Communion, open my eyes, like the eyes of Simeon, that I may see the ways of salvation.

The Finding in the Temple

Dear Mary and Joseph, you shed bitter tears at the loss of your Son. Wash me clean in those tears, and help me to find Jesus in this House of God, and at this table of the Eucharist.

THE SORROWFUL MYSTERIES

The Agony in the Garden

O loving Saviour, by your agony in the Garden; by the sacred sweat of blood; by the great sadness you endured for my sins, I beg you to come to my poor heart in this Holy Communion. O Saviour of the world, I rise and go to meet you.

The Scourging

I adore you, most patient Jesus, bound to a pillar and cruelly scourged. Through the Most Holy Sacrament of your Body and Blood, I wish to make reparation for the terrible injustice done to you, the innocent Lamb who takes away the sins of the world.

The Crowning with Thorns

Sweet Jesus, your sacred head was crowned with sharp thorns. In reparation for the insults and the mockery, I adore you in this Holy Mass, and desire with all my being to make a throne for you in the sanctuary of my heart. Lord, I believe in you; I hope in you; I love you.

The Carrying of the Cross

Come, beloved Saviour, come into my heart. I love you, disfigured and suffering as you are. I wish to receive you and to bind up your wounds. Lamb of God, you take away the sins of the world. Wash the world clean in your Precious Blood.

The Crucifixion
My crucified Jesus, imprint on my soul the wounds of your sacred hands and feet; hide me within your pierced heart. Let me hear those consoling words: 'This day you shall be with me in Paradise'. May this Holy Communion be a foretaste of the heavenly banquet.

The Glorious Mysteries

The Resurrection
Lord, by your Cross and Resurrection you have set us free. You are the Saviour of the world. Like Mary Magdalen at the tomb, seeking your sacred body, I come seeking your face and longing to receive you.

The Ascension
My Divine Jesus, you ascended into Heaven to prepare a place for me; but in this wondrous mystery of the Eucharist you still remain on earth. While awaiting the splendours of heaven, I will find my happiness in adoring you on the altar in your divine humanity.

The Descent of the Holy Spirit
O Mary, in obedience to your Son's command, you once gathered the disciples around you in the Cenacle to prepare for the coming of the Holy Spirit. Gather us, your children, into unity and peace. Prepare us for the 'New Pentecost', and through this Mass make us ready to receive all the gifts and graces the Holy Spirit has in store for us.

The Assumption

O Mary, as we reflect on your assumption into Paradise, may our souls find their Paradise here on earth, around the altar of the Eucharist. From your throne in heaven, dearest Mother, obtain for us the grace to journey safely home in the strength of the 'living bread which comes down from heaven'.

The Coronation of Our Lady

O Queen of Heaven, enthroned in glory, we crown you now with the precious jewels of the life, death and resurrection of Jesus, your Son.

O Jesus, my body pines for you, like a dry weary land without water. So I gaze on you in the sanctuary, to see your strength and your glory.

AFTER MASS OR IN THE PRESENCE OF THE BLESSED SACRAMENT

THE JOYFUL MYSTERIES

The Annunciation

Lord Jesus, I welcome you and open my heart to receive you, as Mary did. Through this celebration of the Eucharist, may I bring you forth as the fruit of my own life and love and labour.

The Visitation

O Jesus, living in Mary, you visit us this day through your priest, as you once visited the hill country of Judah. Fill us, too, with the Holy Spirit, that like Elizabeth we may cry aloud: 'Blessed are you among women, and blessed is the fruit of your womb'.

The Nativity

O Jesus, we believe that you are present with us now, as truly as you lay in the manger. Bethlehem means 'House of Bread'; we thank you for bringing us to this House of God, where you feed us with the bread come down from heaven.

The Presentation in the Temple

Lord Jesus, at the altar of the Jewish temple you were presented to your heavenly Father. We rejoice that, on our altars, you never cease to offer yourself as a victim for humanity. As Simeon took you in his arms and proclaimed you a 'Light to all the people', I take you to my heart that you may enlighten all my ways.

The Finding in the Temple

My Jesus, as Mary and Joseph found you in the Temple, I have found you in your Eucharistic presence. Grant that I may never lose you, but go on day by day seeking to know you more clearly, to follow you more nearly, to love you more dearly.

THE SORROWFUL MYSTERIES

The Agony in the Garden

Lord, the neglect of your presence in this sacrament of love is, surely, an extension of your agony. It is like Gethsemane grown great. May this Holy Communion be a comfort to you in the grief that still overwhelms you in the coldness and indifference of so many of your people.

The Scourging at the Pillar

As I kneel before you, Lord, and remember how you were so cruelly scourged, I ask your forgiveness in the name of all poor sinners. By the Precious Blood which flowed during this bitter torment, cleanse us and help us to drink from the well-springs of salvation in Holy Communion.

The Crowning with Thorns

Sweet Jesus, as I kneel before the tabernacle and adore you within my breast after Communion, I see your thorn-crowned head and behold your beautiful face covered with wounds.

Beloved Lord, I welcome you and make a throne for you in my heart. Grant that I may receive you ever more reverently, and one day be raised up to share your throne in heaven.

The Carrying of the Cross

Dear Lord and Master, I worship you, present before and within me. With heartfelt sorrow, I ponder the heavy load of sin and shame we have laid upon you. Through this Holy Communion, may I bind up your wounds and comfort you.

The Crucifixion

Lord Jesus Christ, Son of the living God, by the will of the Father and the work of the Holy Spirit, your death brought life to the world. By your holy body and blood, free me from all my sins and from every evil. Keep me faithful to your teaching, and never let me be parted from you.

THE GLORIOUS MYSTERIES

The Resurrection

Lord Jesus, I claim your Eucharistic pledge of future glory: He who eats my flesh and drinks my blood has everlasting life, and I will raise him up on the last day.

Through this Holy Sacrament, may I so live on earth that my body may rise, glorious and immortal, on the day of judgment.

The Ascension

O Jesus, the Ascension deprived us of your visible presence here on earth, and a cloud took you out of sight. As you were carried up to heaven, you raised your hands and blessed your disciples. This holy Eucharist brings you back beneath the veils of bread and wine. Raise up your wounded hands now, Lord, and bless us who await your coming back in glory.

The Descent of the Holy Spirit

Father, we have brought you our gifts of bread and wine, and by the power of your Spirit they have become the body and blood of your Son, our Lord Jesus Christ, at whose command we have celebrated this Eucharist. Help us to reap the harvest which the Spirit yields: love, joy, peace, patience, kindness, generosity, faithfulness, gentleness and self-control. (Gal 5:22)

The Assumption

Dear Lord, as I kneel before you in adoration, I ponder your Blessed Mother taken up into heaven, body and soul. Through the saving power of the Eucharist, may I enter one day into the blessed company of Mary and of all the saints and angels, to be in communion with you forever.

The Coronation

O Mary, Queen of the Eucharist, you gave yourself, body and soul, to God, that we might have the living bread come down from heaven. Help us by your prayers to yield our lives also to the transforming power of these sacred mysteries. And after this, our exile, show unto us the blessed fruit of your womb, Jesus.